THE MOST EPIC BASKETBALL STORIES FOR KIDS

Greatest Basketball Players and Games of All Time for Aspiring Young Champions

By Oscar Dasher

Copyright 2024 by Oscar Dasher - All rights reserved.

This document is geared towards providing exact and reliable information in regard to the topic and issue covered. The publication is sold with the idea that the publisher is not required to render accounting, officially permitted, or otherwise, qualified services. If advice is necessary, legal or professional, a practiced individual in the profession should be ordered.

From a Declaration of Principles which was accepted and approved equally by a Committee of the American Bar Association and a Committee of Publishers and Associations. In no way is it legal to reproduce, duplicate, or transmit any part of this document in either electronic means or in printed format. Recording of this publication is strictly prohibited, and any storage of this document is not allowed unless with written permission from the publisher. All rights reserved. The information provided herein is stated to be truthful and consistent, in that any liability, in terms of inattention or otherwise, by any usage or abuse of any policies, processes, or directions contained within is the solitary and utter responsibility of the recipient reader. Under no circumstances will any legal responsibility or blame be held against the publisher for any reparation, damages, or monetary loss due to the information herein, either directly or indirectly.

Respective authors own all copyrights not held by the publisher. The information herein is offered for informational purposes solely and is universal as such. The presentation of the information is without a contract or any type of guaranteed assurance. The trademarks that are used are without any consent, and the publication of the trademark is without permission or backing by the trademark owner. All trademarks and brands within this book are for clarifying purposes only and are owned by the owners themselves, not affiliated with this document.

TABLE OF CONTENTS

INTRODUCTION — 7

CHAPTER 1: THE STILT'S STORY: WILT CHAMBERLAIN'S LEGENDARY CAREER — 9

CHAPTER 2: FROM THE BRINK TO THE GLORY—THE CELTICS 1969 REVIVAL — 18

CHAPTER 3: HOOPS WITHOUT BORDERS—THE HARLEM GLOBETROTTERS ROLE IN NBA INTEGRATION — 28

CHAPTER 4: THE TOWERING TRIUMPH—KAREEM ABDUL-JABBAR AND HIS SCORING RECORD — 37

CHAPTER 5: REGGIE'S REMARKABLE RALLY: OUTDUELING NEW YORK'S FINEST — 44

CHAPTER 6: LAUNCH OF A LEGACY—GAME ONE OF THE ROCKETS 1995 CHAMPIONSHIP BATTLE — 52

CHAPTER 7: LAKERS LEGACY—THE GOLDEN ERA OF SHAQUILLE, KOBE, AND PHIL — 62

CHAPTER 8: TIM DUNCAN THE GENTLEMAN ON THE COURT — 69

CHAPTER 9: HOW NOWITZKI, GINOBILI, AND YAO MING TRANSFORMED BASKETBALL   75

CHAPTER 10: GOLD AND GLORY—THE RISE OF THE 2008 REDEEM TEAM   85

CHAPTER 11: RAPTORS TAKE ON LAKERS IN L.A.   90

CHAPTER 12: CLASH OF TITANS: CLEVELAND VS. GOLDEN STATE IN THE 2016 FINALS   96

CHAPTER 13: MICHAEL JORDAN—A LIVING, BREATHING, WALKING LEGEND   101

CONCLUSION   108

Don't miss out on the **free bonus eBook, A Guide to Basketball Gear and Equipment: Tips for Selecting the Right Shoes, Apparel, and Equipment for Young Basketball Players.**

This power-packed eBook is an absolute must-have for any parent or coach looking to give their rising stars every possible advantage.

We're talking insider secrets on:

- Choosing the perfect basketball shoes to maximize traction, support, and vertical explosion
- Kitting out with ultra-lightweight, moisture-wicking apparel to stay cool and focused
- Selecting the right ball size, backboard height, and essential gear for at-home training

But that's just the warm-up! This guide goes way beyond the basics to cover advanced tips like:

- Identifying the key features in high-performance shoes for guards vs. big men
- Understanding compression technologies to prevent fatigue and muscle strain
- Optimizing your gear for indoor vs. outdoor play

With this eBook as your playbook, you'll be able to suit up with Pro-level knowledge and strategy.

From prolonging the life of your gear to protecting young bodies from injury - it's all here!

Don't let your ballers hit the hardwood at a disadvantage. Get an edge on the competition by claiming your FREE copy of "A Guide to Basketball Gear and Equipment" today! Level up and let's get buckets!

INTRODUCTION

The world will tell you who you are if you let it. It will try to fit you into boxes and tell you what you can and cannot do. But you know what? You are the author of your own story. You get to decide who you are and what you're capable of.

That's what basketball is all about. It's a game that's been around for over a century, but it's always evolving. New players bring new styles and new moves to the game, and each generation has its own legends. But no matter who you are or where you come from, basketball is a game that can help you discover who you are, and what you're capable of.

Maybe you're just getting started with basketball, and you're not sure if you're any good. Maybe you've been playing for years, but you've hit a plateau and you're not sure how to get better. Or maybe you're already a star player, but you're looking for inspiration and motivation to keep pushing yourself to the next level.

Whatever your situation, this book is for you. It's a collection of some of the most epic basketball stories ever told, and they're all aimed at kids just like you. These are stories of triumph and heartbreak, of perseverance and dedication, of teamwork and individual brilliance. They're stories that will make you laugh, make you cry, and make you want to jump up and start playing basketball all right now.

But most importantly, these stories will inspire you. They'll show you that no matter who you are or where you come from, you can achieve great things through basketball. They'll show you that the most important thing is to believe in yourself and your abilities and to work hard every day to make your dreams a reality.

So, be prepared to be mind blown, to learn about some of the greatest basketball players of all time and the amazing things they've accomplished on and off the court. And most importantly, get ready to discover what you're capable of. Because with basketball, anything is possible.

CHAPTER 1: THE STILT'S STORY: WILT CHAMBERLAIN'S LEGENDARY CAREER

"They say that everything is habit forming, so make sure what you do is what you want to be doing"—Wilt Chamberlain

So many of us think that to be good at something you have to have a natural talent for it. I mean, sure, that's something that plays a role, but I think what matters most is the passion and dedication you put into it. Take Wilt Chamberlain, for example. He was a towering figure on and off the basketball court, but his journey to greatness didn't start with innate talent alone.

Imagine a young Wilt, growing up in the streets of Philadelphia. He wasn't born with a basketball in his hands or an extraordinary height that made him stand out from the crowd. In fact, he was just an average kid, like you and me. But what set him apart was his unwavering determination and love for the game.

One day, as Wilt walked home from school, he stumbled upon a basketball court. The sound of sneakers squeaking on the court and the rhythmic thump of the ball caught his attention. Curiosity sparked within him, and he couldn't resist the urge to take a closer look.

As he approached the court, Wilt noticed a group of older kids playing a pickup game. Their moves were mesmerizing, their coordination impeccable. He stood there, captivated by their skill and grace. At that moment, something clicked inside him. He knew he had found his passion.

Without hesitation, Wilt joined the game. He didn't have the fancy moves or the polished technique, but what he lacked in skill, he made up for with sheer determination. He chased after loose balls, fought for rebounds, and never backed down from a challenge. The older kids were impressed by his tenacity, and they soon realized that this lanky, determined young boy had something special.

From that day forward, he dedicated himself to the game of basketball. He practiced tirelessly, honing his skills and pushing himself to the limit. He knew that talent alone wouldn't take him to the top; it was the hours of hard work and unwavering commitment that would set him apart.

And set him apart, he did. Wilt Chamberlain went on to become one of the greatest basketball players of all time. His records and achievements are legendary, but it all started with a young boy who stumbled upon a basketball court and found his passion.

So, I guess what I am trying to say is that greatness is not solely determined by natural talent. It's the love, dedication, and hard work you put into something that truly matters. As we prepare to learn about the career and story of this legend, I hope that you are brave enough to let it inspire you to chase your dreams, no matter where you start.

Wilt: A Summary of Who He Is and Where He Comes From

Born on the 21st of August 1936 in Philadelphia, Pennsylvania, Wilt Chamberlain became a basketball legend who left an indelible mark on the sport. Growing up in a working-class neighborhood, he had a childhood that was far from glamorous or remarkable. The young Wilt faced the same challenges and obstacles that many kids his age did, but what set him apart was his spirit and love for the game.

Standing at a whopping 7 feet 1 inch tall, his height was certainly an advantage on the basketball court. However, we must say and acknowledge that it wasn't just his physical stature that made him a force to be reckoned with. He had an unparalleled combination of strength, agility, and tenacity that set him apart from his peers.

As a young boy, he discovered his passion for basketball by chance. Walking home from school one day, he stumbled upon a basketball court where a group of older kids were playing. Intrigued by the game, he joined in, despite his lack of experience. It was at that moment that Wilt's love affair with basketball began.

Throughout his high school years, his talent on the court became increasingly evident. He dominated the local basketball scene, earning a reputation as an unstoppable force. His incredible athleticism and scoring ability caught the attention of college recruiters, and he was offered a scholarship to play for the University of Kansas.

During his time at Kansas, Wilt's impact on the game was undeniable. He shattered records and set new standards for excellence. His dominance on the court was so profound that it prompted the NCAA to change several rules in an attempt to level the playing field against him.

After his college career, Chamberlain leaped to the professional ranks, joining the Harlem Globetrotters for a brief period before entering the NBA. In the NBA, he played for several teams, including the Philadelphia/San Francisco Warriors, Philadelphia 76ers, and Los Angeles Lakers.

Wilt's professional career was nothing short of extraordinary. He achieved countless accolades, including four regular-season MVP awards, two NBA championships, and seven scoring titles. His scoring prowess was unmatched, and he set numerous records that still stand to this day. Perhaps his most famous achievement was scoring 100 points in a single game—something no one has been able to do since.

Off the court, Wilt Chamberlain was known for his larger-than-life personality and charisma. He was a cultural icon, appearing in movies and television shows, and even releasing a music album. Despite his fame and success, Wilt remained grounded and used his platform to advocate for social causes and inspire future generations.

Wilt Chamberlain's impact on the game of basketball cannot be overstated. He revolutionized the sport with his unmatched athleticism and skill, forever changing the way the game was played. His legacy continues to inspire young athletes like yourself that if you work hard enough, you'll get anywhere you want to be.

Career Highlights

Wilt had some truly incredible moments throughout his career—Curious to know what they are?

Well, first up, we have the scoring records. The guy was a scoring machine, and he holds a record that seems almost impossible to beat. In one game, on March 2, 1962, he scored a mind-boggling 100 points! Can you imagine that? It's like scoring a basket every minute for the entire game. This incredible feat has never been matched by any other player in NBA history.

But that's not all when it comes to scoring. Wilt Chamberlain led the league in scoring for an amazing seven seasons. That means he was the top scorer in the entire NBA, leaving defenders scratching their heads and fans cheering in awe. His ability to put the ball in the basket was simply unmatched.

Now, let's talk about rebounding. He was a force to be reckoned with on the boards. He had a knack for grabbing rebounds like nobody else. In fact, he led the league in rebounds per game for a whopping 11 seasons! That means he was snatching the ball out of the air more often than anyone else. His career average of 22.9 rebounds per game is the highest in NBA history. It's like he had a magnet in his hands!

Of course, being a basketball superstar isn't just about individual achievements. It's also about winning championships. He won not one, but two NBA championships during his career. He helped lead the Philadelphia 76ers to victory in 1967 and then brought home another championship with the Los Angeles Lakers in 1972. The joy of winning it all and celebrating with his teammates must have been an incredible feeling for Wilt.

For his outstanding performances, Wilt Chamberlain was named the NBA Most Valuable Player (MVP) four times. This prestigious award is given to the player who has the biggest impact on their team and the league as a whole. Wilt's dominance on the court was undeniable, and he rightly earned those MVP titles.

Wilt Chamberlain was also a regular at the NBA All-Star Game. He was selected to play in this star-studded event a whopping 13 times! That's like being invited to the coolest basketball party in the world year after year. His skills and popularity among fans and fellow players were truly remarkable.

In recognition of his incredible career, Wilt Chamberlain was inducted into the Naismith Memorial Basketball Hall of Fame in 1978. This is like the ultimate honor for a basketball player. It solidified Wilt's status as one of the greatest players to ever grace the court.

These are just some of the amazing highlights from his career, from his scoring records, rebounding dominance, championships, MVP awards, All-Star appearances, and Hall of Fame induction, these are all that contribute to his legendary status.

Other Records

Wilt was, in a word, phenomenal! So it should come as no surprise to you to hear that there are tons of other records that he holds. Let's have a look at some of those.

- **Single-Season Scoring Average:** Wilt Chamberlain's scoring ability was out of this world. In the 1961-1962 season, he averaged an astonishing 50.4 points per game, a record that still stands today. It's like he had a secret formula for putting the ball in the basket!
- **Career Points:** Over the course of his NBA career, Wilt Chamberlain scored an incredible 31,419 points. That's enough points to fill a basketball encyclopedia! His scoring prowess and longevity in the league allowed him to climb the ranks of the all-time leading scorers.
- **Single-Game Rebounds:** Wilt Chamberlain's dominance extended beyond scoring. He holds the record for the most

rebounds in a single game with a jaw-dropping 55 rebounds. It's like he had a gravitational pull that attracted every missed shot!
- **Career Rebounds:** Throughout his career, Wilt Chamberlain grabbed a staggering 23,924 rebounds. That's enough rebounds to fill a swimming pool! His ability to control the boards was unmatched, as he outmuscled opponents and snatched rebounds with ease.
- **Consecutive Games Played:** Wilt Chamberlain's durability was legendary. He played in an incredible 1,045 consecutive games without missing a single one. It's like he had a superpower that kept him on the court, game after game, inspiring his teammates and fans alike.
- **Field goal percentage:** Wilt Chamberlain holds the record for the highest career field goal percentage in NBA history, shooting an impressive 54.0% from the field. It's like he had a magic touch, with every shot he took.

Lessons To Remember

There is a lot that we can learn from Wilt and his story, incredible lessons that we can use to push and propel us toward our dreams so, here are my all-time favorite lessons that I think each of us can definitely learn from Wilt

- The world doesn't get to decide who you are, you decide. Wilt faced numerous challenges along the way, but what is truly remarkable is that he never let others define his potential. He believed in himself and his abilities, and that self-belief propelled him to greatness.
- Embrace your uniqueness. Wilt Chamberlain was a towering figure on and off the basketball court, but it wasn't just his height that made him special. He embraced his unique

attributes and used them to his advantage. We all have something that sets us apart, and embracing our individuality can lead to extraordinary achievements.

- Hard work beats talent when talent doesn't work hard. Wilt's success was not solely based on natural talent alone. He understood the importance of hard work and dedication. He put in countless hours of practice and pushed himself to the limit, always striving to improve. This work ethic is a valuable lesson for all of us.
- Never back down from a challenge. Wilt Chamberlain never shied away from competition or difficult situations. He faced some of the greatest players of his time head-on, never backing down from a challenge. This fearless attitude allowed him to grow and excel in the face of adversity.
- Set ambitious goals and chase them relentlessly. Wilt set his sights on achieving greatness, and he pursued his goals with unwavering determination. He didn't settle for mediocrity but instead aimed for the stars. Setting ambitious goals and working tirelessly towards them can lead to extraordinary accomplishments.
- Be a team player. Despite his individual brilliance, Wilt Chamberlain understood the importance of teamwork. He recognized that success is often achieved through collaboration and supporting those around you. Being a team player and lifting others up can create a positive and winning environment.
- Leave a lasting legacy. Wilt Chamberlain's impact on the game of basketball is undeniable. He left a lasting legacy that continues to inspire generations of players. His story reminds us of the importance of leaving our own mark, whether it's in sports, academics, or any other field. Strive to make a positive impact and leave a legacy that will be remembered.

As we wrap up this chapter, I hope that you open up your heart and allow these lessons to inspire you to believe in yourself, embrace your uniqueness, work hard, face challenges head-on, set ambitious goals, be a team player, and strive to leave a lasting legacy. Wilt's story is a testament to the power of determination, passion, and perseverance. Let it fuel your own journey towards greatness.

CHAPTER 2: FROM THE BRINK TO THE GLORY—THE CELTICS 1969 REVIVAL

My grandfather was a great Celtics fan. Man, I wish you could hear and see the pride in his eyes when he talked about the first basketball game he ever went to! I am going to try and retell it as best as I can so here goes.

"I had just turned 12," he told me, a twinkle in his eye as he recalled that momentous day. "It was a crisp winter evening, and the excitement in the air was palpable. The year was 1968, and little did I know that I was about to witness a game that would forever change my love for the Celtics."

As my grandfather continued his story, I could feel the anticipation building. He described how the crowd filled the arena, their cheers echoing through the rafters. The atmosphere was electric, and he couldn't help but be swept up in the energy of the moment. "The players took to the court, and the game began," he said, his voice filled with nostalgia. "The speed, the skill, the sheer intensity of the game—

it was like nothing I had ever seen before. But what truly captivated me was the unwavering spirit of the Celtics."

He recounted how the Celtics faced a formidable opponent that night, a team that seemed to have the upper hand. The game was a back-and-forth battle, with both teams leaving everything on the court. The tension was palpable, and the outcome hung in the balance.

"But just when it seemed like all hope was lost, the Celtics rallied," my grandfather continued, a smile spreading across his face. "They dug deep, finding a reserve of strength and determination that was truly awe-inspiring. Their teamwork, their resilience—it was a sight to behold!"

In the final moments of the game, the Celtics made a jaw-dropping comeback. They fought tooth and nail, refusing to let defeat overshadow their spirit. The crowd erupted in thunderous applause as the final buzzer sounded, signaling a hard-fought victory for the Celtics.

"That game taught me a valuable lesson," my grandfather said, his voice filled with wisdom. "It showed me that no matter how dire the circumstances may seem, with perseverance and a never-give-up attitude, you can overcome even the toughest challenges."

As I listened to my grandfather's story, I couldn't help but feel a surge of admiration for the Celtics and their remarkable journey. Their 1968-1969 season would go down in history as a challenging but rewarding one, filled with moments of triumph and resilience.

Little did I know that this game my grandfather spoke of was just the beginning of an incredible season for the Celtics. As I delved deeper into their story, I discovered the trials they faced, the obstacles they overcame, and the glory they ultimately achieved. It was a season that would forever be etched in the annals of basketball history.

And so, as we are about to start another chapter, I hope that we can continually think about the spirit of the Celtics, their unwavering determination, and the valuable lessons we can learn from their journey. From the brink of adversity to the sweet taste of glory, their story is a testament to the power of resilience and teamwork.

The Celtics: A Brief History of Who They Were

The Celtics, one of the most storied teams in NBA history, have a rich and illustrious past that spans decades. They were founded in 1946 and are based in Boston, Massachusetts. The team's iconic logo features a leprechaun, a symbol associated with Irish folklore and luck.

From their early years, it was evident that they were a force to be reckoned with. Led by legendary coach Red Auerbach, the team quickly became known for their fast-paced, team-oriented style of play. They emphasized selflessness, ball movement, and strong defense, which set them apart from other teams.

They experienced their first taste of success in the 1950s and 1960s. During this era, they assembled a formidable lineup that included legendary players such as Bill Russell, Bob Cousy, and John Havlicek. Together, they formed a dynasty that dominated the NBA, winning an unprecedented 11 championships in 13 seasons from 1957 to 1969.

What made them truly great was their unparalleled teamwork and chemistry. They epitomized the concept of "team basketball," with players sacrificing personal glory for the greater good of the team. Their selfless play and relentless determination earned them the admiration of fans across the country. Their success continued into the 1970s and 1980s, with the emergence of new stars like Larry Bird, Kevin McHale, and Robert Parish. This era saw the Celtics win three more championships in 1981, 1984, and 1986, solidifying their status as one of the greatest teams in NBA history.

Throughout their history, the Celtics have been known for their passionate fan base and the electric atmosphere at their home games in the iconic TD Garden. The team's green and white colors have become synonymous with Boston sports and are proudly worn by fans around the world. Beyond their on-court success, they have also been at the forefront of social change. Bill Russell, in particular, used his platform to advocate for civil rights and challenge racial inequality, making a lasting impact both on and off the court.

Today, they continue to be just as great, just as an incredible force in the NBA, with a tradition of excellence that is carried on by a new generation of players. They embody the values of hard work, teamwork, and resilience, inspiring young fans to dream big and pursue their goals.

Challenges

Now it's no secret that the Celtics faced a bit of a rollercoaster ride during their 1968-1969 season. They encountered various challenges that tested their resilience and determination. Let's take a closer look at some of these hurdles:

- **Transition period**: The Celtics were going through a transition phase during this season. Many of their key players from the previous championship-winning years had retired or were nearing the end of their careers. This meant that the

team had to integrate new players and find a way to maintain their winning culture.
- **Injuries:** Throughout the season, the Celtics had to deal with injuries to key players. These injuries disrupted team chemistry and forced the remaining players to step up and fill the void. It was a test of their depth and ability to adapt to changing circumstances.
- **Strong competition:** The NBA was filled with talented teams during this era, making the competition fierce. The Celtics had to face formidable opponents like the Los Angeles Lakers, Philadelphia 76ers, and New York Knicks, who were all vying for the championship. Each game was a battle, and the Celtics had to bring their A-game to come out on top.
- **Fatigue and exhaustion:** They had enjoyed a remarkable run of success in the previous years, which took a toll on their players both physically and mentally. The constant pressure to perform at a high level and the demanding schedule of the NBA season left them fatigued. Overcoming this exhaustion and finding the motivation to push through was a significant challenge.
- **Internal struggles:** Like any team, they had their fair share of internal struggles. There were disagreements, egos, and clashes of personalities that had to be managed. Maintaining team cohesion and unity in the face of these challenges was crucial to their success.

Despite these obstacles, they never lost sight of their ultimate goal. They embraced the challenges as opportunities to grow and improve. They leaned on their experience, leadership, and the winning culture that had been established over the years to navigate through the tough times. This ability to overcome, this resilience is exactly what we all need. It was a testament to the team's character and the unwavering belief they had in themselves and each other.

Memorable Moments

Everyone, whether it's a sports star or an individual pursuing their passion, will have a defining moment that changes the whole trajectory of their career. It's like in the movie "Akeelah and the Bee," where a young girl's journey takes an unexpected turn when she discovers her hidden talent for spelling.

In the world of basketball, the Celtics had their own unforgettable moment that altered the course of their 1968-1969 season. It was a game that would go down in history as one of the most thrilling and iconic moments in Celtics lore.

Picture this: They were facing their arch-rivals, the Los Angeles Lakers, in a high-stakes matchup. The tension in the air was palpable as the two teams battled fiercely on the court. The game was neck-and-neck, with both sides refusing to give an inch.

As the clock ticked down, the Celtics found themselves trailing by a single point. The pressure was mounting, and the outcome of the game hung in the balance. It was a moment that would test the Celtics' mettle and define their season.

With just seconds remaining, they inbounded the ball. The crowd held their breath as the play unfolded. The ball found its way into the hands of one of the Celtics' star players, who had already showcased his clutch performances throughout the season.

In a split second, he made a move that left the defenders in awe. With a burst of speed and finesse, he drove to the basket, maneuvering through a sea of defenders. Time seemed to stand still as he soared through the air, defying gravity, and released a shot that seemed destined to decide the game's outcome.

The ball arced through the air, and the crowd erupted in anticipation. It seemed like an eternity before the ball finally found its mark—nothing but net. The arena exploded in a thunderous roar as the Celtics took the lead in the dying seconds of the game. That unforgettable shot became an indelible moment in Celtics history. It was a testament to the team's resilience, skill, and unwavering determination. It ignited a fire within the Celtics, propelling them to further success and inspiring generations of fans.

Now, let's explore some of the other memorable moments that defined the Celtics' 1968-1969 season. From incredible comebacks to record-breaking performances, these moments showcased the team's greatness and left an indelible mark on the annals of basketball history.

- **The Return of Bill Russell**: After briefly retiring at the end of the previous season, Celtics legend Bill Russell made a dramatic comeback. His return brought a renewed sense of leadership and defensive prowess to the team, inspiring his teammates and fans alike.
- **John Havlicek's heroics**: John Havlicek, known for his hustle and clutch performances, had several memorable moments throughout the season. His ability to come through in crucial moments, whether it was hitting a game-winning shot or making a key steal, solidified his status as one of the Celtics' all-time greats.
- **Record-breaking performance**: On November 15, 1968, they played against the New York Knicks in a game that would go down in history. In that game, the Celtics set an NBA record by scoring 173 points, the highest single-game total in league

history at the time. It was a remarkable offensive display that showcased the team's scoring prowess.

- **Overcoming the Lakers:** The rivalry between the Celtics and the Lakers reached new heights during the 1968-1969 season. The two teams faced each other multiple times, engaging in intense battles that captivated fans. The Celtics' ability to consistently come out on top against their fierce rivals showcased their mental toughness and competitive spirit.
- **Playoff triumph:** Their journey in the playoffs was filled with memorable moments. They faced tough opponents like the Philadelphia 76ers and the New York Knicks, but they persevered and advanced to the NBA Finals. Their resilience and ability to rise to the occasion in high-pressure situations were on full display throughout the postseason.
- **The ultimate victory:** In the NBA Finals, they faced off against the Los Angeles Lakers in a thrilling series. The teams battled fiercely, but in the end, the Celtics emerged victorious, capturing their 11th championship in 13 seasons. It was a crowning achievement that solidified their dynasty and cemented their place in basketball history.

Key Players of The Season

The Celtics' 1968-1969 team featured several key players who played pivotal roles in their success. Here are some of the standout players from that season.

1. **John Havlicek:** Known for his versatility and relentless work ethic, Havlicek was a vital player for the Celtics. He contributed both offensively and defensively, showcasing his scoring ability, playmaking skills, and tenacious defense. Havlicek's clutch performances and ability to rise to the occasion made him a cornerstone of the team.

2. **Bill Russell**: A legendary figure in Celtics history, Russell returned from a brief retirement to lead the team once again. As a dominant defensive force, Russell anchored the Celtics' defense with his shot-blocking and rebounding prowess. His leadership and basketball IQ were invaluable to the team's success.
3. **Sam Jones**: A prolific scorer and a key member of the Celtics' dynasty, Jones provided a consistent offensive threat. He had a smooth shooting stroke and a knack for scoring in clutch moments. Jones's ability to deliver in pressure situations made him a crucial component of the team's success.
4. **Bailey Howell**: A skilled forward, Howell brought versatility and scoring ability to the lineup. He was known for his rebounding prowess and his ability to score from both inside and outside the paint. Howell's contributions on both ends of the court were instrumental in the team's success.
5. **Don Nelson**: Nelson was a versatile player who provided a spark off the bench. He was known for his hustle, basketball IQ, and ability to make timely plays. Nelson's energy and contributions in various aspects of the game made him an important asset to the team.
6. **Emmette Bryant:** Bryant was a strong presence in the frontcourt. He provided rebounding and defensive stability, using his size and strength to battle against opponents in the paint. Bryant's contributions on the boards and his defensive presence were valuable to the team's success.

Lessons To Remember

Every season has a lesson, and the most important ones that I want you to take away from the Celtics are these.

- **Teamwork makes the dream work:** Just like the Celtics, working together with your teammates can lead to success. Support each other, communicate effectively, and collaborate to achieve your goals.
- **Never give up:** The Celtics faced challenges but never lost hope. Remember, perseverance is key. Keep pushing forward, even when things get tough.
- **Practice makes perfect:** The Celtics honed their skills through practice and dedication. Whether it's sports, academics, or hobbies, consistent practice can help you improve and reach your full potential.
- **Stay resilient:** Like the Celtics, be resilient in the face of setbacks. Learn from failures, bounce back stronger, and keep moving forward.
- **Believe in yourself:** Confidence is crucial. Trust in your abilities, set goals, and believe that you have what it takes to succeed.
- **Embrace Challenges:** Challenges can be opportunities for growth. Don't shy away from them; instead, face them head-on and learn from the experience.
- **Celebrate successes:** Just as the Celtics celebrated their victories, remember to acknowledge and celebrate your achievements, no matter how big or small.
- **Support your teammates:** Offer support and encouragement to your peers. Lift each other up, celebrate each other's successes, and be there for one another in times of need.
- **Learn from failure:** Mistakes happen, and that's okay. Use them as learning opportunities, analyze what went wrong, and use that knowledge to improve in the future.
- **Have Fun:** Lastly, remember to enjoy the journey. Just like the Celtics found joy in playing the game they loved, find joy in what you do, and have fun along the way.

CHAPTER 3: HOOPS WITHOUT BORDERS— THE HARLEM GLOBETROTTERS ROLE IN NBA INTEGRATION

As kids, my friends and I called the basketball court our dream playground. Those afternoons we spent passing hoops and balls weren't just about shooting baskets; they were about friendship, competition, and the joy of the game. One summer day, as the sun beat down on the asphalt court, we found ourselves in the midst of an epic showdown. The teams were chosen, the rules were set, and the game was on.

I remember the sound of sneakers squeaking on the court, the rhythmic thump of the ball hitting the ground, and the cheers and jeers of my friends echoing in the air. We played with passion and intensity, each of us channeling our inner basketball hero as we dribbled, passed, and shot our way to victory.

As the game reached its climax, the score was tied, and tensions ran high. It was a moment of pure adrenaline, where every dribble, every pass, and every shot mattered. And then, in a flash of brilliance, my friend pulled off a move straight out of a Harlem Globetrotters playbook.

With a twirl, a spin, and a behind-the-back pass that left us all in awe, he orchestrated a play that seemed to defy the laws of physics. The ball danced through the air, finding its way into the waiting hands of our teammate, who sank the winning shot with seconds to spare.

The court erupted in cheers and high-fives as we celebrated our victory. But beyond the thrill of winning, that moment sparked something within us—a newfound appreciation for the artistry and showmanship of basketball. It was a reminder that basketball was more than just a game; it was a form of expression, a way to connect with others, and a source of inspiration.

Little did we know that our humble game on the asphalt court was a reflection of a much larger story unfolding in the world of basketball. A story that involved pioneers who broke barriers, challenged norms, and paved the way for a more inclusive and diverse sport. And, at the heart of that story were the Harlem Globetrotters, whose impact on the game transcended boundaries and brought people together in ways that went beyond the court.

The Globetrotters: A Brief History of Who They Were

The Harlem Globetrotters are like basketball superheroes who have been playing the game in a fun and entertaining way since the 1920s. They started in Chicago, where they faced challenges because of unfair rules that kept African American players from competing with others. At first, the team played serious basketball, but they soon added tricks, jokes, and amazing moves to their games. People loved watching them because they were not only great players but also super funny and talented.

Even though they had to deal with tough times because of racism, they showed everyone that teamwork, skill, and friendship are what really matters in sports. They broke down barriers and inspired others to believe in themselves, no matter what obstacles they faced.

The team's name comes from Harlem, a cool neighborhood in New York City known for its rich history and culture. The Globetrotters brought Harlem's spirit of creativity, joy, and togetherness to basketball courts around the world, making people smile and cheer wherever they went. From incredible dribbling tricks to unbelievable shots, they have amazed audiences with their skills and showmanship. They've encouraged both kids and adults to have fun, work hard, and always support each other, both on and off the court.

In a world where barriers still exist, the Harlem Globetrotters stand as a shining example of how sports can transcend differences, bring people together, and inspire positive change. Their impact on basketball and society at large serves as a testament to the transformative power of sports and the enduring legacy of those who dare to dream, defy expectations, and make a difference.

Their Impact On Basketball

Back in the old days, when basketball was just starting to become a big deal, there were some unfair rules that kept African American players from showing off their skills on the court. These rules created barriers and made it hard for everyone to play together, no matter how talented they were. But then, along came the Harlem Globetrotters, a team of basketball wizards who changed the game in more ways than one. Let's see how these basketball heroes made a difference and broke down those barriers with style and flair!

- **Integration pioneers:** The Harlem Globetrotters were like superheroes who fought against unfair rules and showed everyone that talent knows no boundaries. They opened doors for African American players and paved the way for a more inclusive and diverse basketball world.
- **Entertainment and showmanship:** The team didn't just play basketball; they put on a show! With their amazing tricks, fancy moves, and hilarious antics, they made the game fun and exciting for fans of all ages.
- **Global ambassadors:** Traveling around the world, they really shared the joy of basketball with people everywhere. They showed that sports can bring us together, no matter where we come from or what we look like.
- **Influence on playing style:** The Globetrotters' fast-paced, creative style of play inspired a whole new generation of basketball players. Their teamwork, skill, and passion set the bar high for what basketball could be.
- **Inspiration for future generations:** The one thing they showed us is that with hard work, determination, and a little bit of fun, we can achieve anything. They taught us that sports are about more than just winning; they're about unity, friendship, and believing in ourselves.

Memorable Moments

- **The Magic Circle:** One of the Globetrotters' signature moves is the "Magic Circle," where players pass the ball around in a mesmerizing display of teamwork and skill. This dazzling routine has wowed audiences around the world and become a fan favorite at Globetrotters' games.

- **The half-court shot**: The team is known for their incredible trick shots, and one of the most jaw-dropping feats is the half-court shot. Watching a player sink a basket from halfway across the court never fails to amaze fans and showcase the team's extraordinary shooting abilities.
- **The confetti bucket**: This one is a classic moment where a player sneaks a bucket of confetti onto the court and surprises everyone by dumping it over an opponent's head after scoring a basket. This playful prank adds a touch of humor and fun to the game.
- **The four-point shot**: In a display of skill and showmanship, they introduced the four-point shot, a shot taken from beyond the traditional three-point line. This high-risk, high-reward move adds an extra element of excitement to their games and keeps fans on the edge of their seats.
- **The theme song**: Every Globetrotters game kicks off with their iconic theme song, "Sweet Georgia Brown." The catchy tune sets the stage for an action-packed and entertaining performance, getting fans pumped up and ready for an unforgettable show.
- **The Trotter Tunnel**: Before each game, the Globetrotters make a grand entrance through the "Trotter Tunnel," a high-energy procession that gets the crowd cheering and sets the tone for a fun-filled experience. This interactive tradition allows fans to connect with the players and feel like part of the Globetrotters family.
- **The Globetrotters' Harlem Shake**: Putting their own spin on the viral dance craze, the Globetrotters created their version of the "Harlem Shake," a fun and lively routine that showcases their creativity and sense of humor. This playful dance has become a fan favorite and a must-see moment at Globetrotters' games.

- **The Globetrotters' victory dance:** Celebrating a win in style, the team always breaks out into a victory dance that is as entertaining as their gameplay. With moves that range from silly to spectacular, the team's post-game celebrations are a joyous display of camaraderie and sportsmanship.
- **The unmatched generosity:** Beyond their on-court performances, they are known for their philanthropic efforts and community outreach. From visiting children's hospitals to supporting charitable causes, the team's commitment to giving back and making a positive impact off the court is a memorable aspect of their legacy.
- **Their legacy:** As ambassadors of goodwill and sportsmanship, the team has left a lasting legacy that transcends basketball. Their ability to bring people together, spread joy, and inspire others to dream big and have fun is a testament to the enduring impact of their remarkable history.

What Makes Them So Entertaining?

Every person or every team has characteristics that define them. These are the things that set them apart and would make you recognize them in an instant. For the Harlem Globetrotters, it's a unique combination of skill, humor, tradition, and community spirit that makes their games so entertaining for fans. Let's dive into what makes the Globetrotters' games a must-see experience for audiences of all ages:

- **Their skillful craftsmanship:** The Globetrotters' games are filled with mind-blowing basketball tricks that showcase their exceptional talent and athleticism. From dazzling dribbling displays to unbelievable trick shots, their skillful maneuvers leave fans in awe of their mastery of the game.

- **Their humorous antics:** In addition to their impressive basketball skills, the Globetrotters bring humor and comedy to the court, infusing their games with playful pranks, funny routines, and entertaining interactions that keep the audience laughing and engaged throughout the game.
- **Interactive fan engagement:** The Globetrotters go beyond the court to engage with their fans, inviting audience members to participate in on-court activities, dance-offs, and interactive challenges that create a fun and inclusive atmosphere for everyone in attendance.
- **Signature traditions:** From their iconic theme song, "Sweet Georgia Brown," to their unique pre-game rituals like the "Trotter Tunnel" entrance, the Globetrotters' games are steeped in tradition and nostalgia, providing fans with a sense of familiarity and excitement.
- **High-energy performances:** Their games are nothing short of boring and are known for their high-energy performances, featuring fast-paced gameplay, acrobatic moves, and electrifying dunks that keep fans on the edge of their seats and create a dynamic and thrilling experience for spectators.
- **Innovative gameplay:** With their innovative and unconventional approach to basketball, they introduce new elements to their games, such as the four-point shot and creative trick plays, that push the boundaries of traditional basketball and keep fans guessing what they'll do next.
- **Cultural impact:** Beyond the entertainment value, the Globetrotters' games carry a deeper significance, resonating with fans through their rich history of breaking down barriers, promoting diversity, and inspiring unity among people from all walks of life.

Lessons on Humanity From The GlobeTrotters

- **Embrace diversity:** People are people, and their worth should never be defined by external factors like race, ethnicity, or appearance. Embracing diversity and recognizing the value of each individual's unique qualities enriches our communities and fosters understanding and respect.
- **Practice empathy:** Putting yourself in someone else's shoes and understanding their experiences can cultivate empathy and compassion. By listening, supporting, and showing kindness to others, we create a more empathetic and caring world where everyone feels seen and valued.
- **Celebrate differences:** Our differences make us unique and should be celebrated rather than feared. Embracing diversity in all its forms, whether cultural, social, or personal, enriches our lives and broadens our perspectives, fostering a more inclusive and accepting society.
- **Stand up against injustice:** When we witness injustice or discrimination, it's important to speak up and take action. Standing up for what is right, advocating for equality, and challenging unfair treatment can help create a more just and equitable world for all.
- **Promote unity:** Building bridges and fostering connections among diverse groups promotes unity and understanding. By coming together, sharing experiences, and working towards common goals, we can break down barriers, promote harmony, and create a sense of belonging for everyone.
- **Practice kindness:** Small acts of kindness can have a big impact on others. Whether it's a smile, a helping hand, or a word of encouragement, practicing kindness towards others fosters a sense of community, builds trust, and spreads positivity in the world.

- **Listen and learn:** Listening to others' stories, experiences, and perspectives can broaden our understanding of the world and help us grow as individuals. By being open-minded, curious, and willing to learn from others, we can expand our horizons and cultivate a deeper sense of empathy and connection.
- **Be an ally:** Being an ally means actively supporting and advocating for marginalized or underrepresented groups. By using our voice, privilege, and resources to uplift others, we can work towards a more inclusive and equitable society where everyone has the opportunity to thrive and succeed.

CHAPTER 4: THE TOWERING TRIUMPH— KAREEM ABDUL-JABBAR AND HIS SCORING RECORD

You know I have met a lot of people in my life, each of whom has played a monumental role in my life and the one person that I want to single out right now is a basketball coach from our school. He also happened to be the gym teacher, and I remember how he just liked to give us these little pep talks in between sessions. I remember the one day he told us, "Guys, you can't be a winner if you don't know how to lose. This was a rather confusing statement. I won't lie.

I remember the puzzled look on our faces as we tried to make sense of Coach's words. "You can't be a winner if you don't know how to lose," he repeated, his eyes twinkling with wisdom. It was like a light bulb went off in my head. The coach wasn't just talking about basketball; He was talking about life. He explained that losing teaches us resilience, humility, and the determination to keep pushing forward. It's not about the setbacks we face but how we bounce back from them that truly defines us. It's about learning from our failures, growing stronger, and never giving up on our dreams.

As I reflected on Coach's words, I realized that he wasn't just teaching us about basketball; He was teaching us about life. He showed us that success isn't just about winning. It's about the journey, the lessons learned, and the character we build along the way.

Coach's pep talks became more than just words. They became guiding principles that shaped how I approached challenges, setbacks, and victories. He taught me that true success isn't measured by the number of wins but by the resilience, determination, and growth we experience through both wins and losses.

So, as we are about to dig into the story of Kareem Abdul-Jabbar and his legendary scoring record, keep these words in mind because they very much represent who Kareem was.

A Brief History of Kareem

Kareem Abdul-Jabbar, born Ferdinand Lewis Alcindor Jr. on April 16, 1947, in New York City, would go on to become one of the greatest basketball players in history. Raised in Manhattan, He discovered his love for basketball at an early age, towering over his peers and showcasing exceptional skills on the court.

When he was in high school at Power Memorial Academy in New York, he dominated the basketball scene, leading his team to multiple championships and earning a reputation as a prodigious talent. Standing at an impressive 7 feet 2 inches tall, his combination of size, skill, and agility set him apart from his peers and caught the attention of college recruiters across the country.

In 1965, he started college at the University of California, Los Angeles (UCLA), under the guidance of coach John Wooden. It was at UCLA where Kareem, still known as Lew Alcindor at the time, made a lasting impact on the college basketball landscape. His dominance on the court was unparalleled, leading the UCLA Bruins to three consecutive NCAA championships from 1967 to 1969.

After his college career, he went to the professional ranks after being selected as the first overall pick in the 1969 NBA Draft by the Milwaukee Bucks It was here that he adopted the name, Kareem Abdul-Jabbar, reflecting his embrace of Islam and his commitment to social justice and civil rights causes. His entry into the NBA marked the beginning of something great for him; Something that would span two decades and solidify his status as one of the game's all-time greats.

Known for his signature skyhook shot, footwork, and basketball IQ, Kareem revolutionized the center position and became a scoring machine, dominating opponents with his finesse and skill.

Throughout his NBA career, he earned several accolades, including six NBA championships, six MVP awards, and a record-breaking 38,387 points scored, making him the league's all-time leading scorer. Beyond his on-court achievements, His impact extended off the court, where he used his platform to advocate for social justice, civil rights, and education.

IT GeTS BeTTer: STaying AT The Top

I think we all know that if you aren't willing to work hard, you won't achieve that much or get to where you want to be. It's like the saying goes, "Hard work pays off," and that's exactly what Kareem Abdul-Jabbar showed us throughout his incredible basketball career. Let's dive into the exciting story of Kareem's championship victories and

All-Star appearances in a way that will make you feel like you're right there in the action.

Imagine this—It's the NBA Finals, and the Milwaukee Bucks are facing off against the Baltimore Bullets. The tension is high, the crowd is roaring, and Kareem Abdul-Jabbar is in the zone. With his trademark skyhook shot and unstoppable moves, Kareem led the Bucks to their first NBA championship in 1971. The crowd goes wild as Kareem hoists the trophy high, a symbol of his hard work and dedication paying off in the ultimate victory.

But the success didn't just stop there. In the years that followed, he continued to dominate the court, leading the Bucks and later the Los Angeles Lakers to multiple NBA championships. His skill, leadership, and determination propelled his teams to greatness, solidifying his legacy as a true basketball legend.

Not only was Kareem a force to be reckoned with in the championships, but he also shone brightly in the NBA All-Star games. Picture this: It's the NBA All-Star weekend, and the best players in the league have gathered for a showcase of talent and skill. Among them stands Kareem Abdul-Jabbar, a towering figure with unmatched finesse and grace on the court.

Year after year, his numerous All-Star selections as he dazzled fans with his scoring prowess, shot-blocking abilities, and basketball IQ. His All-Star appearances were not just about individual accolades but a testament to his impact on the game and his status as one of the league's premier players.

Some other honorable achievements that he also got throughout his career include

- he won the NBA MVP award a record six times during his career, showcasing his dominance and impact on the game.

- he was selected to the NBA All-Defensive Team multiple times, highlighting his defensive prowess and shot-blocking abilities.
- he led the NBA in scoring multiple times, demonstrating his scoring prowess and offensive skills.
- Kareem Abdul-Jabbar retired as the NBA's all-time leading scorer with 38,387 points, a record that still stands today.
- in recognition of his outstanding career, he was inducted into the Naismith Memorial Basketball Hall of Fame in 1995.
- in his debut season, Kareem Abdul-Jabbar was named the NBA Rookie of the Year, setting the stage for a remarkable career ahead.
- he was named NBA Finals MVP twice, underscoring his impact in leading his teams to championship success.
- beyond his on-court achievements, Kareem Abdul-Jabbar used his platform to advocate for social justice, civil rights, and education, leaving a lasting impact on and off the basketball court.

A New Standard For Greatness

Greatness is not just about individual achievements on the basketball court, but also about the impact that you as a player have on the culture around them. Abdul was not only a dominant force in the NBA, but he also had a profound cultural significance that set a new standard for greatness.

His impact on the culture of basketball and society as a whole was unforgettable. As a young player, he faced racial discrimination and adversity, but he persevered and used his platform to advocate for social justice and equality. He embraced his Muslim faith and became a voice for religious tolerance and understanding. His cultural significance extended beyond the court, as he also used his influence to inspire and empower others to stand up for what they believe in.

Yes, his achievements on the court were remarkable, but it was his ability to transcend the game of basketball and make a lasting impact on society that truly set him apart. His legacy is not just about his scoring records and championship victories, but about the way he challenged the status quo and paved the way for future generations of athletes to use their platform for positive change.

In setting a new standard for greatness, he showed that being a great athlete is not just about physical prowess, but also about using one's influence to make a difference in the world. He demonstrated that athletes have the power to effect change and inspire others, and he set a high bar for what it means to be truly great both on and off the court.

Jabbar's cultural significance and his new standard for greatness serve as a powerful example for young readers. His story teaches them that greatness is not just about individual accomplishments, but also about the impact they have on the world around them. It encourages them to use their talents and influence to make a positive difference and to strive for greatness in all aspects of their lives. Abdul Kareem Jabbar's legacy will continue to inspire and challenge future generations to redefine what it means to be truly great.

Final Notes on Humility

I think there is a lot that we can learn about humility from Kareem, especially after having just read about who he is and what he represents, here's what I have learned and I hope that there is something that you can take away; something that resonates with you.

- It's okay to be proud of your achievements, but remember that humility allows you to connect with others and be more relatable.
- Humility means recognizing your strengths while also acknowledging the contributions of others to your success.
- Being humble doesn't mean downplaying your talents; it means using them to lift others up and make a positive impact.
- It's being open to learning from others and understanding that everyone has something valuable to offer.
- True humility is about being confident in your abilities while also showing respect and empathy towards others.
- Humility allows you to accept and learn from your mistakes, and to grow and improve as a person.
- Remember, humility is not about thinking less of yourself, but about thinking of yourself less and focusing on the needs and feelings of others.

CHAPTER 5: REGGIE'S REMARKABLE RALLY: OUTDUELING NEW YORK'S FINEST

I've asked people who have been part of a team what their favorite part of being on a team was, and the responses I received were truly inspiring. One person shared that their favorite part was the sense of camaraderie and belonging that came with being part of a team. They talked about how the shared goals and experiences created a bond that went beyond just playing a game together. Another mentioned that their favorite part was the opportunity to learn from others and grow as a player and as a person. They spoke about how being on a team taught them about teamwork, leadership, and perseverance.

Someone else shared that their favorite part was the feeling of support and encouragement that they received from their teammates. They talked about how, during tough games or challenging moments, their teammates were always there to lift them up and keep them going. It made them feel like they were part of something bigger than themselves, a community that had each other's backs no matter what.

One response that stood out was from someone who mentioned that their favorite part was the thrill of coming together as a team to achieve a common goal. They talked about the excitement of working together, strategizing, and celebrating victories as a unified group. The sense of accomplishment and pride in their collective efforts was something they cherished deeply.

As I read through these responses, I couldn't help but think about how these sentiments perfectly capture the essence of what it means to be part of a team. The connections, the growth, the support, and the shared victories all contribute to a powerful and meaningful experience. In the world of basketball, there are countless stories that exemplify these sentiments, one of which belongs to the legendary Reggie Miller. His remarkable rally and the impact he had on his team and the sport as a whole is a testament to the true spirit of teamwork and resilience.

Reggie Miller: Who He Was

Reggie Miller was a basketball superstar who made a lasting impact on the sport. He was born on August 24, 1965, in Riverside, California, and grew up in a family that was passionate about basketball. His older sister, Cheryl Miller, was a basketball legend herself, and Reggie looked up to her as a role model.

His journey in basketball began when he was a young boy. He started playing basketball in his backyard and quickly fell in love with the game. His passion for basketball grew as he played in local leagues and school teams. Reggie's height and shooting skills set him apart on the court, and he soon gained a reputation for his sharpshooting abilities. As he continued to hone his skills, he caught the attention of college scouts. He went on to play for the University of California, Los Angeles (UCLA), where he made a name for himself as a standout player. During his time at UCLA, he showcased his incredible talent and work ethic, earning recognition as one of the top collegiate players in the country.

In 1987, Reggie was selected by the Indiana Pacers in the NBA Draft, marking the beginning of his professional basketball career. He quickly made a name for himself as a prolific scorer, known for his three-point shooting and clutch performances. Reggie's sharpshooting abilities and his knack for scoring in crucial moments earned him the nickname "Knick Killer" due to his memorable performances against the New York Knicks, one of the Pacers' biggest rivals.

Throughout his career, he became known for his competitive spirit and his ability to lead his team to victory. He was not only a skilled athlete but also a respected leader on and off the court. His dedication to the sport and his team made him a beloved figure in the basketball world.

He inspired countless young athletes and basketball fans like yourselves with his tenacity, sportsmanship, and dedication to the game. His legacy is something that continues to inspire others to dream big and pursue their passion for basketball.

Memorable Moments

Reggie Miller's career was filled with memorable moments that solidified his status as a basketball legend. Known for his sharpshooting abilities and clutch performances, Miller left an indelible mark on the sport. Here are some of his most iconic and unforgettable moments throughout his career.

- **Eight Points in Nine Seconds:** One of Reggie Miller's most legendary moments came during the 1995 NBA Playoffs. In a crucial game against the New York Knicks, Miller scored eight points in the final nine seconds of the game, leading the Indiana Pacers to a stunning victory. His remarkable scoring spree showcased his ability to perform under pressure and solidified his reputation as a clutch player.
- **Rivalry with the New York Knicks:** Reggie Miller's rivalry with the New York Knicks became the stuff of basketball lore. His competitiveness and memorable performances against the Knicks, both in the regular season and playoffs, captivated fans and solidified his status as a formidable opponent. His battles with the Knicks, particularly against players like John Starks and Patrick Ewing, became the stuff of basketball legend.
- **Scoring Milestones:** Throughout his career, Reggie Miller achieved numerous scoring milestones that showcased his scoring prowess and longevity in the NBA. He surpassed the 25,000 career points mark, further solidifying his place among the greatest scorers in NBA history. His consistent ability to score from beyond the arc and in clutch moments made him a feared offensive threat.
- **Three-Point Shooting Records:** Reggie Miller was renowned for his exceptional three-point shooting abilities. He set multiple records for three-pointers made in a game and held the record for the most three-point field goals made in NBA history at the time of his retirement. His precision from long range and his ability to knock down crucial three-pointers during pivotal moments of games made him a true marksman.
- **All-Star Performances:** Reggie Miller was a five-time NBA All-Star, showcasing his elite skills and earning recognition as one of the top players in the league. His performances in

All-Star games highlighted his scoring ability and his impact on the game, further solidifying his place among the basketball elite.

Reggie Miller's career was defined by his remarkable ability to rise to the occasion and deliver unforgettable moments on the basketball court. His competitiveness, skill, and clutch performances cemented his legacy as one of the greatest players in NBA history. His enduring impact on the sport continues to be celebrated by fans and aspiring basketball players around the world.

The Iconic Play-Off

In the final quarter of the 1995 NBA Playoffs game between the Indiana Pacers and the New York Knicks, Reggie Miller delivered one of the most memorable and exhilarating performances in basketball history. With the Pacers trailing and the team's hopes on the line, Miller unleashed a scoring barrage that left an indelible mark on the sport.

The game was a high-stakes playoff matchup that captivated fans and showcased the intense rivalry between the Pacers and the Knicks. The tension in the arena was palpable as the two teams battled it out on the court. With the Knicks holding a lead, Miller knew that he needed to elevate his game and lead his team to victory.

As the final quarter unfolded, Miller's competitive fire ignited, and he rose to the occasion with unparalleled determination. With the crowd roaring and the pressure mounting, Miller displayed his sharpshooting prowess and strategic precision. With the ball in his hands, he capitalized on the Knicks' errors with surgical precision, seizing every opportunity to narrow the gap and propel the Pacers forward.

In a sequence that would go down in basketball history, Miller faced off against the Knicks' John Starks, engaging in an iconic duel that showcased their competitive spirit and skill. As the clock ticked down, Miller's three-point shooting prowess came to the fore, as he unleashed a series of successive three-pointers that electrified the crowd and propelled the Pacers back into contention. Each shot was a testament to Miller's sharpshooting abilities and his ability to perform under pressure.

Amidst the intense gameplay, the courtside interactions between Miller and the Knicks' fan-favorite, Spike Lee, added another layer of drama to the unfolding spectacle. Spike Lee's animated presence and vocal support for the Knicks only fueled Miller's competitive fire, as he thrived under the pressure and rose to the occasion with unwavering focus and determination.

As the game reached its climax, Miller's scoring barrage and unwavering resilience captivated fans and left an indelible mark on the sport. His performance against the Knicks showcased his ability to thrive in high-pressure situations and solidified his reputation as a clutch player. The game led to a thrilling victory for the Pacers, with Miller's heroic performance etched into basketball history as a shining example of skill, resilience, and unwavering competitive spirit.

One of the most valuable lessons we can learn from this incredible performance in the 1995 NBA Playoffs is the power of tenacity and the ability to thrive under pressure. The guy's remarkable display of skill and unwavering competitive spirit serves as a very good example of how we can overcome obstacles and rise to the occasion in the face of daunting challenges.

His ability to maintain focus and deliver exceptional performance in a high-stakes, pressure-filled environment shows us just how mental toughness and composure are important. His sharpshooting abilities and strategic precision under pressure highlight the significance of honing one's skills and staying calm in critical moments. The game serves as a reminder that adversity can be an opportunity for us to showcase our talents and push beyond our limits.

Let's not forget about the duel with John Starks and his interactions with Spike Lee, those show us the impact of competitive spirit and the role of external motivation in driving our performance. The dynamic between Miller, his opponents, and the passionate crowd exemplifies the influence of external factors on an individual's drive and determination.

Fun Facts About Reggie

1. Reggie Miller is known for his love of movies and has made cameo appearances in several films, including "Forget Paris" and "He Got Game."
2. In addition to basketball, Reggie Miller also has a passion for golf and has participated in celebrity golf tournaments.
3. Reggie Miller has a unique pre-game ritual where he chews on his mouthguard during games for good luck and focus.
4. During his NBA career, Reggie Miller was known for his trash-talking on the court, often engaging in banter with opponents to gain a mental edge.
5. Reggie Miller is an avid philanthropist and has been involved in various charitable initiatives, including supporting children's health and education programs.
6. Miller holds the record for the most career points scored in the playoffs without winning an NBA championship, showcasing his individual scoring prowess.

7. Reggie Miller has a keen interest in fashion and has been noted for his stylish and distinctive wardrobe choices off the court.
8. Miller's sister, Cheryl Miller, is a basketball Hall of Famer and an Olympic gold medalist, making basketball a prominent part of their family's legacy.
9. Reggie Miller is a fan of the Indiana Hoosiers college basketball team and has been seen cheering them on during games.
10. In retirement, Reggie Miller transitioned to a successful career as a basketball analyst and commentator, providing insights and analysis on NBA games and events.

These fun facts offer a glimpse into the diverse interests and experiences of Reggie Miller beyond his basketball career, showcasing different facets of his personality and life outside the sport.

CHAPTER 6: LAUNCH OF A LEGACY—GAME ONE OF THE ROCKETS 1995 CHAMPIONSHIP BATTLE

Remember the story that I told you in an earlier chapter of how my Grandfather experienced his first live basketball game at age eleven, well I have another story for you, this one is of how a friend of mine met his wife at a basketball game. He tells it all the time with as much detail as my grandfather and with a little glimmer in his eyes.

My friend vividly recalls the crisp autumn evening when he first laid eyes on his wife, the radiant glow of the stadium lights casting a warm aura over the court. It was a pivotal game, a clash of titans that had drawn a fervent crowd eager to witness the unfolding drama. As he settled into his seat, his anticipation mingled with the electric energy pulsating through the air, setting the stage for a moment that would alter the course of his life.

The game surged with intensity, each play igniting the crowd's fervor as the players weaved through the court with precision and grace. And then, amid the symphony of cheers and the rhythmic bounce of the ball, he caught sight of her. She was a vision of elegance and poise, her eyes ablaze with an infectious passion for the game. As fate would have it, their eyes met in a serendipitous exchange, and in that fleeting moment, a timeless connection was forged.

It was during a nail-biting overtime, the tension palpable, that he found himself drawn to her infectious enthusiasm for the game. Their shared elation with every basket and every defensive stand kindled an unspoken bond, transcending the confines of the court. As the final buzzer sounded, marking a hard-fought victory for the home team, he seized the opportunity to approach her, his heart racing with a blend of nervousness and anticipation.

Their conversation flowed effortlessly, their shared love for basketball serving as a poignant backdrop to a blossoming connection. As they exchanged stories of their favorite players and memorable games, the stadium's bustling energy faded into the background, leaving only the resonance of their shared laughter and the promise of something extraordinary.

In the years that followed, their love deepened and flourished, rooted in the magic of that encounter at the basketball game. Their shared passion for the sport became a cornerstone of their relationship, a solidified bond that moved beyond time and circumstance. As my friend recounts this tale with a glimmer in his eyes, it serves as a testament to the transformative power of basketball, weaving together the threads of destiny and love in a tapestry of cherished memories.

So, you see, the legacy of basketball moves beyond the boundaries of the court, intertwining with the fabric of our lives and shaping the narratives that define us. As we dive into the next chapter, we'll witness how the game's legacy unfolds in the most unexpected and extraordinary ways, leaving an indelible mark on the hearts and lives of those who embrace its enduring magic.

A Brief History of The Houston Rockets

The Houston Rockets are a professional basketball team that has been a powerhouse in the NBA for many years. They are based in Houston, Texas, and have a rich history filled with thrilling moments and remarkable achievements. The Rockets have been an integral part of the NBA, moving fans with their electrifying performances and unwavering spirit.

One of the most exciting things about them is their dynamic style of play. They are known for their fast-paced, high-scoring offense, which often leads to thrilling games filled with intense action and jaw-dropping plays. The team's commitment to pushing the boundaries of the game and creating exhilarating moments on the court has made them a favorite among basketball enthusiasts.

The Rockets have also been home to some of the most iconic players in NBA history. From legendary players like Hakeem Olajuwon and Clyde Drexler to modern stars like James Harden and Yao Ming, the Rockets have consistently showcased exceptional talent and skill. These players have not only left an indelible mark on the team's legacy but have also contributed to the overall excitement and allure of the NBA.

In addition to their on-court prowess, they have a devoted fan base that passionately supports the team. The energy and enthusiasm of their fans create an electric atmosphere at every game, turning the Toyota Center into a cauldron of excitement and fervor. Their loyal supporters, known for their unwavering dedication, play an essential role in fueling the team's competitive drive and adding to the vibrant tapestry of the NBA.

The Rockets have also made a significant impact off the court through their community engagement and philanthropic initiatives. They are committed to making a positive difference in the lives of others, whether it's through charitable efforts, youth development programs, or community outreach. The team's dedication to giving back and uplifting their community reflects their values and their desire to inspire positive change beyond the realm of basketball.

Not to forget, their pursuit of excellence extends beyond their impact in Houston. They have a rich history of competing at the highest levels of the NBA, earning accolades and championships that have solidified their status as a formidable force in the league. Their resilience, determination, and unwavering pursuit of greatness have left an enduring imprint on the NBA landscape, inspiring generations of basketball enthusiasts around the world.

Commencement of The 1995 NBA Finals

The Houston Rockets' journey to the 1995 NBA Finals was nothing short of amazing. They had battled through the playoffs, facing tough opponents and overcoming formidable challenges to earn their spot in the championship series. As they stepped onto the grand stage of the NBA Finals, they were determined to defend their title and etch their names in basketball history once again.

The opening game of the 1995 NBA Finals set the tone for a series that would showcase their spirit. The atmosphere in the arena crackled with anticipation as the Rockets squared off against their formidable opponents, ready to unleash their trademark intensity and tenacity on the court. The energy was electric, and the crowd's roar echoed through the stadium, fueling the Rockets' resolve as they prepared to embark on their quest for glory.

From the opening tip-off, you could see their relentless drive and unshakeable determination. They attacked the game with unbridled passion, executing dazzling plays and showcasing their exceptional teamwork. Every pass, every shot, and every defensive stand spoke to their commitment to excellence, igniting a firestorm of excitement and anticipation in the hearts of their fans.

As the game unfolded, the Rockets' determination became the focal point of a captivating battle on the court. They faced formidable challenges and formidable opponents, but they refused to back down, summoning their collective strength and skill to overcome every obstacle in their path. The intensity of the game reached a fever pitch, and the Rockets' unwavering resolve shone brightly, illuminating the path to victory with each breathtaking moment.

In the end, they emerged triumphant as champions, securing a pivotal victory in the opening game of the 1995 NBA Finals. Their resounding win set the stage for a series that would rock the basketball world and leave a mark on the annals of NBA history. Their unshakeable spirit and their unyielding pursuit of greatness had ignited a spark that would burn brightly throughout the finals, propelling them toward a legacy-defining triumph.

The opening game of the 1995 NBA Finals set the stage for a series that would showcase their mesmerizing skill. It was a stirring commencement that would ultimately mark their place in basketball history, leaving an enduring legacy that continues to inspire and captivate basketball enthusiasts around the world.

Remembering Remarkable Plays

In the 1995 NBA Finals, the Rockets showed their incredible skills and teamwork. Hakeem Olajuwon, a legend in the basketball world, played a huge role in the Rockets' success. He was a force to be reckoned with in the paint, using his size and skill to dominate the game. Olajuwon's ability to score and defend near the basket made him a key player for the Rockets.

Clyde Drexler, a veteran player with a lot of experience, brought his savvy and leadership to the team. His basketball smarts and ability to make big plays helped guide the Rockets through the intense competition of the finals. Drexler's presence on the court gave the team a boost, and his contributions were crucial to the Rockets' success.

The Rockets also had role players like Robert Horry, who made a big impact with his clutch shooting. Horry's ability to come through in crucial moments, sinking important shots when the pressure was on, was a game-changer for the Rockets. His contributions were instrumental in the team's victory, and his presence on the court added depth and strength to the Rockets' lineup.

Throughout the finals, the Rockets' teamwork and determination were on full display. They worked together seamlessly, combining their individual talents to create a formidable force on the court. The team's chemistry and cohesion were evident in every play, as they supported each other and executed their game plan with precision and skill.

Also, They had some truly unforgettable moments that showed their talent and determination. One of the most memorable moments came from Hakeem Olajuwon, the Rockets' star center. Olajuwon dominated the series with his incredible skills in the paint, scoring points and defending the basket with finesse. His performance in

Game 1, where he scored 34 points and grabbed 11 rebounds, set the tone for the entire series. Olajuwon's ability to take over games and lead the Rockets to victory was a sight to behold and remains a highlight of the 1995 Finals.

Another standout moment came from Clyde Drexler, a veteran player known for his leadership and basketball IQ. Drexler's experience and savvy were on full display in Game 3, where he made crucial plays that helped the Rockets secure a pivotal win. His ability to come through in clutch moments and guide the team through the intense competition of the Finals was a key factor in the Rockets' success.

The 1995 NBA Finals also saw the emergence of role players like Robert Horry, whose contributions were instrumental in the Rockets' victory. Horry's clutch shooting in Game 7, where he sank several crucial shots in the fourth quarter, proved to be a game-changer for the Rockets. His ability to step up when the pressure was on and make big plays was a defining moment in the series, showcasing the depth and strength of the Rockets' lineup.

One of the most thrilling moments of the Finals came in Game 4 when the Rockets faced a tough challenge against their opponents. The game went into overtime, and the Rockets showed their resilience and never-say-die attitude as they battled fiercely to secure a hard-fought victory. The team's commitment to excellence was on full display, captivating fans and leaving an indelible mark on the series. These memorable moments of the 1995 Finals, from Olajuwon's dominance in the paint to Drexler's veteran leadership and Horry's clutch shooting, continue to inspire and captivate basketball enthusiasts, showcasing the enduring legacy of the Houston Rockets.

Awards

During the 1995 NBA season, the Houston Rockets achieved remarkable success, and their players received several prestigious awards in recognition of their outstanding performances. These accolades highlighted the individual talents and contributions of the Rockets' star players, further cementing their place in basketball history.

Hakeem Olajuwon, the Rockets' legendary center, received the NBA Most Valuable Player (MVP) award for the 1993-1994 season. This honor recognized Olajuwon's exceptional skills, leadership, and impact on the Rockets' success. As the MVP, Olajuwon's dominant presence in the paint, scoring prowess, and defensive prowess were crucial in leading the Rockets to victory and solidifying his status as one of the greatest players in NBA history.

In addition to the MVP award, Hakeem Olajuwon was also recognized for his stellar defensive abilities by being named the NBA Defensive Player of the Year for the 1993-1994 season. This award highlighted Olajuwon's extraordinary prowess as a defender, his shot-blocking expertise, and his ability to anchor the Rockets' defense. His defensive prowess was a key factor in the Rockets' success, and this accolade underscored his impact on the team's performance.

Clyde Drexler, a veteran player known for his leadership and basketball IQ, was also honored during the 1995 NBA season. Drexler received the NBA Sportsmanship Award, which recognized his exemplary conduct on and off the court. This award highlighted Drexler's integrity, respect for the game, and positive influence as a role model for aspiring basketball players. Drexler's leadership and sportsmanship were integral to the Rockets' success, and this accolade underscored his positive impact on the team and the broader basketball community.

Their success during the 1995 NBA season was also reflected in their All-NBA Team selections. Hakeem Olajuwon and Clyde Drexler were both named to the All-NBA First Team, recognizing their splendid performances and impact on the league. These selections highlighted the individual talents and contributions of Olajuwon and Drexler, further solidifying their status as elite players in the NBA. In addition to these individual accolades, their collective achievements during the 1995 NBA season were also recognized through their impressive team performance. The way they stuck to the goal, and their exceptional teamwork, helped them get to their place of victory, culminating in their second consecutive NBA championship.

Lessons on Bouncing Back

- I think that one of the most important or most significant things that we can learn from basketball is the spirit of bouncing back. There will always be setbacks, things that hold us back but I think that if we're in the right mindset, we can pull ourselves together again and make our way to the top again. As we wrap up this chapter here are a few things that I want you to keep in mind; lessons that you must keep with you and take as you navigate life and all of its messy twists and turns.
- You don't have to be the strongest person to bounce back. Just the most courageous. Courage is what carries and sustains us when the what-if voices get too loud.
- Failure is not the end; It's an opportunity for growth and learning. Welcome it and allow it to be your teacher that provides valuable lessons. It's through our failures that we gain insight, develop new skills, and build the determination

to persevere. Every setback is a chance to refine our approach and emerge stronger than before.
- Focus on the possibilities and opportunities that lie ahead, and maintain a hopeful outlook even in the midst of adversity. A positive mindset can fuel your resilience and propel you forward.
- Draw strength from the people who surround you. This will make the journey more manageable and uplifting.
- Don't be rigid. Be open. Embrace flexibility and adaptability as you navigate through the twists and turns. Being open to change and willing to adjust your approach can help you navigate challenges with resilience and agility.
- Be kind to yourself as you bounce back from setbacks. You aren't a loser or worthless. Acknowledge your emotions, be gentle with yourself, and celebrate your progress, no matter how small. Self-compassion nurtures resilience and fosters a sense of inner strength.
- Keep moving forward with the same determination and perseverance you started with. Setbacks may slow you down, but they don't have to stop you. Stay focused on your goals, take consistent steps toward progress, and remember that each step forward, no matter how small, brings you closer to success.

CHAPTER 7: LAKERS LEGACY—THE GOLDEN ERA OF SHAQUILLE, KOBE, AND PHIL

Basketball as you can tell from all the stories that I've shared has played a big role in my life. Any chance that I got to talk about it, you better believe I grabbed at that opportunity. Like show and tell in fifth grade I used this as an opportunity to show off my basketball trading cards to the entire class. I was so proud of my collection, and I remember vividly how I excitedly explained the stats and achievements of each player to my classmates. It was a moment that solidified my love for the game and sparked a passion for basketball that has stayed with me throughout my life.

One particular memory that stands out is the time I attended my first live NBA game. I was around 10 years old, and my parents surprised me with tickets to see the Los Angeles Lakers play at the Staples Center. As a young fan, I was ecstatic at the prospect of witnessing my basketball heroes in action.

The energy and anticipation in the arena were palpable as the game began. The crowd erupted with cheers as the players took the court, and I was swept up in the electric atmosphere. The Lakers' iconic purple and gold jerseys glistened under the arena lights, and I felt a surge of excitement as the game unfolded before my eyes.

As the game went on, I was completely engrossed in the on-court action, marveling at the athleticism and skill of the players. The swish of the net, the thunderous dunks, and the precision of the players' movements left me in awe. I was captivated by the sheer intensity and artistry of the game, and I felt a deep connection to the sport that went beyond mere fandom.

Seeing the game live was a changing experience that deepened my appreciation for basketball. It was more than just a game; it was a captivating display of talent, teamwork, and sheer determination. The Lakers' legacy and the indelible impact of their golden era were on full display, and I was fortunate to witness it firsthand.

That experience at the Staples Center left an indelible impression on me, solidifying my passion for basketball and igniting a lifelong admiration for the sport. It was a moment that shaped my love for the game and reinforced the enduring legacy of the Lakers, setting the stage for the captivating journey that lay ahead.

Kobe

Kobe Bryant was a legendary figure in the world of basketball, known for his unparalleled skill, mind, heart, and fire for the sport. Born on August 23, 1978, in Philadelphia, Pennsylvania, Kobe's early years were shaped by his deep love for basketball. He was the son of former NBA player Joe "Jellybean" Bryant, and from a young age, Kobe was immersed in the world of basketball, learning the nuances of the game from his father.

His passion for basketball blossomed as he honed his skills and developed a relentless work ethic. His talent and dedication were evident early on, and he quickly established himself as a standout player. During his high school years at Lower Merion High School in Ardmore, Pennsylvania, Kobe garnered widespread attention for his exceptional abilities on the court. His remarkable talent and scoring prowess set the stage for a remarkable journey in basketball.

In 1996, his path to stardom took a significant turn when he declared for the NBA draft after graduating from high school. At just 17 years old, he was selected by the Charlotte Hornets as the 13th overall pick. However, in a landmark trade, Kobe was subsequently traded to the Los Angeles Lakers, where he would begin his illustrious career. This pivotal moment marked the beginning of a transformative chapter for both Kobe and the Lakers, setting the stage for an extraordinary legacy to unfold.

His arrival in Los Angeles heralded the emergence of a basketball prodigy who would leave an indelible mark on the sport. As a young player, Kobe's talent, work ethic, and unwavering determination set him apart. He quickly became known for his fearlessness on the court, his scoring prowess, and his relentless pursuit of excellence. His partnership with Shaquille O'Neal, another basketball luminary, would come to define an era of dominance for the Lakers, culminating in multiple NBA championships and a lasting legacy for both players.

The impact he had on the Lakers and the broader basketball community was profound, and his journey from a young phenom to a basketball icon continues to inspire fans and aspiring athletes around the world. His passion for the game, his unyielding pursuit of greatness, and his enduring legacy as a player and a leader have left and set some remarkable standards for the world of basketball.

Shaquille O'Neal

Shaquille O'Neal, often referred to as Shaq, is a towering figure in the history of basketball. Born on March 6, 1972, in Newark, New Jersey, Shaquille's journey to basketball stardom began at an early age. His remarkable combination of size, strength, and agility set the stage for a career marked by dominance and sheer athleticism.

After a standout college career at LSU, Shaquille's arrival in the NBA was met with great anticipation. In the 1992 NBA Draft, he was selected as the first overall pick by the Orlando Magic. His impact was immediate, and he quickly established himself as one of the most formidable forces in the league.

In 1996, Shaquille O'Neal made a pivotal move that would forever alter the landscape of basketball. He signed with the Los Angeles Lakers, marking the beginning of a transformative era for the franchise. Shaq's arrival in Los Angeles brought a seismic shift in the team's dynamics, ushering in a new era of dominance and championship aspirations.

Shaquille's impact on the Lakers was nothing short of monumental. His imposing presence on the court, coupled with his unparalleled skill and athleticism, elevated the team to new heights. His partnership with Kobe Bryant, another rising star, formed a formidable duo that would come to define an era of Lakers basketball.

Together, Shaq and Kobe propelled the Lakers to unprecedented success, clinching multiple NBA championships and solidifying their status as basketball icons. Shaquille's dominance in the paint, his scoring prowess, and his ability to command the attention of opposing defenses made him an indispensable asset to the Lakers' lineup.

Off the court, Shaquille O'Neal's larger-than-life personality and charisma endeared him to fans worldwide. His impact extended beyond the game of basketball, as he became a cultural phenomenon and a beloved figure in the sports world.

Shaquille O'Neal's tenure with the Lakers left an enduring legacy, and his influence on the team's history is undeniable. His contributions to the franchise, both on and off the court, set the stage for an era of unparalleled success and cemented his status as a basketball legend.

Phil Jackson

Phil Jackson, often referred to as the "Zen Master," is renowned for his distinctive coaching philosophy and his remarkable ability to manage and motivate talented but sometimes contentious personalities within a team. His coaching journey is marked by a unique blend of leadership, mindfulness, and a deep understanding of the human psyche, which has left an indelible mark on the world of basketball.

Phil Jackson's coaching career began to take shape in the late 1980s when he assumed the head coaching role for the Chicago Bulls. His tenure with the Bulls coincided with the emergence of Michael Jordan as a basketball icon, and under Jackson's guidance, the team achieved unprecedented success. Jackson's coaching philosophy, influenced by his studies of Eastern philosophy and Native American spirituality, emphasized mindfulness, teamwork, and a holistic approach to the game.

Jackson's ability to manage and motivate the talented but sometimes contentious personalities on the Bulls, including Michael Jordan and Scottie Pippen, was a testament to his unique coaching acumen. He fostered an environment of trust, respect, and open communication, allowing players to flourish while maintaining a cohesive team dynamic.

In 1991, he led the Bulls to their first NBA championship, marking the beginning of a remarkable coaching legacy. His emphasis on mindfulness, mental fortitude, and the cultivation of a collective team spirit became hallmarks of his coaching style and set the stage for a transformative era in basketball.

Following his success with the Bulls, Phil Jackson's coaching prowess continued to shine as he transitioned to the Los Angeles Lakers. His arrival in Los Angeles heralded the start of another golden era in Lakers basketball, as he guided a roster brimming with talent, including Shaquille O'Neal and Kobe Bryant, to multiple NBA championships.

Jackson's ability to manage the dynamic personalities on the Lakers roster, including the formidable duo of Shaq and Kobe, underscored his exceptional leadership and coaching skills. His emphasis on mindfulness, harmony, and a shared sense of purpose fostered an environment where individual talents coalesced into a cohesive, championship-winning team.

Throughout his coaching journey, his distinctive approach to the game, rooted in mindfulness, teamwork, and a deep understanding of human dynamics, set him apart as a visionary leader in the world of basketball. His coaching philosophy and his ability to manage and motivate talented but sometimes contentious personalities have left an enduring legacy that continues to resonate in the annals of basketball history.

Lakers Achievements

1. **Championships:** The Lakers have won a total of 17 NBA championships, which is tied with the Boston Celtics for the most in NBA history.
2. **Hall of Fame players:** The Lakers have been home to some of the greatest players in basketball history, including Magic Johnson, Kareem Abdul-Jabbar, Jerry West, Shaquille O'Neal, Kobe Bryant, and many others.
3. **Longest Winning streak:** The Lakers hold the record for the longest winning streak in NBA history with 33 consecutive wins during the 1971-72 season.
4. **Showtime era:** The 1980s Lakers, led by Magic Johnson and Kareem Abdul-Jabbar, were known for their fast-paced, high-scoring style of play dubbed "Showtime." They won five championships during this era.
5. **Three-Peat:** The Lakers achieved a three-peat by winning three consecutive championships in 2000, 2001, and 2002 with a roster featuring Shaquille O'Neal and Kobe Bryant.
6. **Kobe Bryant's legacy:** Kobe Bryant, one of the greatest players in Lakers history, won five championships with the team and left a lasting impact on the franchise and the game of basketball.

CHAPTER 8: TIM DUNCAN THE GENTLEMAN ON THE COURT

Okay, so I want you to bear with me. I know that you know that I love my anecdotes, but my grandfather used to give me a whole lot of pep talks about building good habits. But I think that my favorite one yet was on what it means to be a gentleman. I remember my dad sternly telling me, "Son, being a gentleman is not just about opening doors for people or saying 'please' and 'thank you.' It's about how you treat others, on and off the court."

I didn't fully understand what he meant at the time, but as I grew up and became more involved in basketball, I started to see the importance of his words. One player who embodied this idea of being a gentleman on the court was a true inspiration to me. He was a quiet and unassuming player, but his impact on the game of basketball was undeniable.

As I watched him play, I saw how his demeanor and sportsmanship set him apart from other players. His conduct on and off the court was a true embodiment of what my dad had talked about. He was respectful to his teammates, opponents, and coaches, always conducting himself with humility and grace.

This player's leadership and gentlemanly conduct earned him the respect of his peers and fans alike. His dedication to the game, coupled with his humble and respectful nature, served as a reminder that true sportsmanship is just as important as skill and talent. And that, my friends, is the mark of a true gentleman on the court.

Tim Duncan: A Brief History of Who He Was

Tim Duncan, also known as "The Big Fundamental," was an icon who spent his entire career with the San Antonio Spurs. He was born and raised in the U.S. Virgin Islands, where he first discovered his love for basketball. Despite facing personal tragedy at a young age, losing his mother when he was just 14, he found a sense of purpose in the game of basketball.

When he was growing up, he excelled in a lot of sports, including swimming and basketball. However, it was his raw talent and dedication to basketball that eventually led him to pursue a career in the sport. After a massive growth spurt in his teenage years, he began to take basketball more seriously and caught the attention of college scouts.

He attended Wake Forest University, where he continued to hone his skills and develop into a dominant force on the court. His outstanding performances and sportsmanship earned him the reputation of being a true gentleman of the game. It was during his college years that he earned the nickname "The Gentleman" for his calm and respectful demeanor both on and off the court.

When he transitioned to the professional level, joining the San Antonio Spurs as the first overall pick in the 1997 NBA Draft. The impact he had was immediate. His work ethic, talent, and gentlemanly approach to the game helped lead the Spurs to multiple championships. He became a role model for young basketball players everywhere, showing that success on the court could be achieved with integrity and respect. The one thing we can also say is that his legacy as a gentleman on the court continues to inspire young athletes to this day. His humble and respectful nature reminds us that true sportsmanship is just as important as skill and talent.

His Remarkable Achievements

Tim Duncan's humble and respectful nature set him apart in the world of professional basketball, making him not only a great player but also an incredible role model for fans, teammates, and aspiring athletes alike. Despite his mind-blowing talent and several accomplishments on the court, he stayed grounded, approachable, and focused on teamwork rather than personal glory.

His humility was evident in his demeanor both on and off the court. He was known for his quiet and unassuming personality, preferring to let his performance speak for itself rather than seeking attention or accolades. He consistently deflected praise to his teammates and coaches, emphasizing the importance of collaboration and unity in achieving success. This respectful nature that he embodies extends beyond his interactions with his fellow players and coaches. Duncan treated everyone with kindness and respect, from the team's equipment managers to the fans who supported him throughout his career. He conducted himself with dignity and integrity, earning the admiration and respect of his peers and fans across the league.

Despite his superstar status, he never really chased after the spotlight or allowed his success to go to his head. He remained dedicated to his craft, putting in the work day in and day out to improve his game and help his team succeed. His work ethic and commitment to excellence served as an inspiration to those around him, encouraging them to strive for greatness in their own efforts

In addition to his exemplary character, his on-court achievements further solidified his legacy as one of the greatest players in NBA history. Throughout his illustrious career with the San Antonio Spurs, Duncan amassed an impressive list of accolades and accomplishments, including:

- Five-time NBA champion (1999, 2003, 2005, 2007, 2014)
- Three-time NBA Finals MVP
- Two-time NBA MVP (2002, 2003)
- 15-time NBA All-Star
- 15-time All-NBA Team selection
- 15-time NBA All-Defensive Team selection
- NBA Rookie of the Year (1998)
- One of the greatest power forwards in NBA history

All of these things are what distinguished him as a true basketball legend and role model for generations to come. That's basically your kids, and your children's kids, and so forth.

Lessons on Character

There are tons of valuable lessons that we can learn from Tim, but I also think that one of the things that truly stands out is what we can learn about his character. Here are some important lessons on character that I hope you can take and carry with you for a long time.

- Character is consistent. It is not defined by a single act or moment of success but by the consistent choices and actions you make day in and day out. It is about staying true to who

you are in all circumstances, even when faced with challenges or adversity.
- Humble in victory. Gracious in defeat. How you handle success and failure says a lot about your character. Showing humility in victory and grace in defeat demonstrates strength of character, resilience, and respect for the game and your opponents.
- Integrity is a key ingredient. Upholding your integrity means staying true to your values, being honest and ethical in all your dealings, and doing the right thing even when no one is watching. Integrity is the foundation of trust and respect in any relationship.
- It is about empathy and compassion as well. Showing empathy and compassion towards others is a sign of strength, not weakness. Understanding and caring for the feelings and experiences of others fosters connection, kindness, and a sense of community.
- Facing challenges, setbacks, and failures with resilience and determination can build character and inner strength. Perseverance teaches you to keep going, learn from your experiences, and grow stronger in the face of adversity.
- It's about having the courage to stand up for what is right. Character is also about having the courage to stand up for your beliefs, speak out against injustice, and advocate for what is right, even when it is difficult or unpopular. Courageous actions can inspire others and make a positive impact on the world.
- Character is generous too. Sharing your time, resources, and talents with others in need not only benefits those around you but also enriches your own life. Generosity and giving back reflect a generous spirit, kindness, and a commitment to making a difference in the lives of others.

- It requires you to know yourself. Self-awareness and a willingness to reflect on your actions, behaviors, and attitudes can help you identify areas for growth and improvement. Striving to become the best version of yourself through self-reflection and continuous learning is a key aspect of building strong character.

CHAPTER 9: HOW NOWITZKI, GINOBILI, AND YAO MING TRANSFORMED BASKETBALL

So you may probably be way too young to even remember this, but when I was much younger we had these gum that came in multicolored wrappers and when you'd unfold the wrapper, there'd be one or another fun fact about some random topic. Oh boy, I used to collect them like I was going to get paid for my collection of stick paper.

For me, my jackpot moment was when I found a wrapper that had a basketball fact in it. I was so excited that day, I must have read over the text a hundred times I mean do you blame me? The fun fact on that the gum wrapper was like a hidden treasure waiting to be discovered. It talked about the magic of basketball, the thrill of the game, and the way it brought people together. I couldn't get enough of it, soaking in every word like it was a secret code to unlock a whole new world.

As I read and reread that fact, something stirred inside me. It wasn't just about bouncing a ball and shooting hoops; it was about passion, dedication, and the power of teamwork. The more I delved into the world of basketball, the more I realized its transformative impact on players and fans alike. That wrapper became my gateway to a universe where giants roamed the courts, where underdogs defied the odds, and where legends were born. It sparked a curiosity in me, and a hunger to learn more about the game and the incredible individuals who shaped its history.

Little did I know that beyond those colorful wrappers and fun facts lay a world where players like Nowitzki, Ginobili, and Yao Ming would leave an indelible mark on the sport. Their stories were woven with threads of resilience, talent, and a deep love for the game that transcended borders and boundaries. I honestly realize now that it was more than just a piece of trivia. It was one of the many sparks that ignited my passion for basketball, a passion that would lead me to write about the sport and the extraordinary players who helped shape its legacy. Okay, I think that's enough storytelling for now, let's get to the good stuff about these star players.

Dirk Nowitzki

Dirk Nowitzki, a basketball icon from Germany, made his mark on the NBA, particularly during his tenure with the Dallas Mavericks. He was born in Wurzburg, Germany, and his journey to the NBA began in 1998 when he was selected by the Milwaukee Bucks as the ninth overall pick in the NBA Draft. However, he was swiftly traded to the Mavericks on draft night, setting the stage for a legendary career.

He is known for his exceptional shooting and versatility as a power forward. His unique skill set, which combined size, shooting accuracy, and ball-handling abilities, revolutionized the power forward position. Fans marveled at his signature one-legged fadeaway jumper, a move that became synonymous with his name. When he joined the Mavericks, he wasted no time in making his mark. His impact on the team was immediate, and he soon emerged as a fan favorite. The incredible work ethic that he had, and his incredible leadership qualities endeared him to both teammates and fans alike. His humility and team-first mentality set him apart as a true ambassador of the game.

One of the defining moments of Nowitzki's career came in 2011 when he led the Mavericks to their first NBA championship. His stellar performance throughout the playoffs, culminating in a Finals MVP award, solidified his legacy as one of the greatest players in NBA history. Nowitzki's clutch performances and unwavering determination during the championship run endeared him to basketball fans worldwide. Beyond his on-court achievements, Nowitzki's impact extended to philanthropic endeavors and community involvement. His charitable work and contributions off the court further solidified his status as a role model and ambassador for the sport.

Throughout his illustrious 21-season NBA career, Nowitzki amassed numerous accolades, including 14 All-Star selections, the 2007 NBA MVP award, and an NBA Finals MVP award. He also became the first European-born player to reach the 30,000-point milestone, underscoring his scoring prowess and longevity in the league. His impact on the Dallas Mavericks organization and the NBA as a whole cements his status as a true legend of the game.

Notable Moments From His Career

Dirk Nowitzki's career is filled with memorable games and moments that have solidified his legacy as one of the greatest players in NBA history. Some standout games and moments include:

- **2011 NBA Finals:** Nowitzki led the Dallas Mavericks to their first NBA championship by defeating the Miami Heat in a thrilling series. His clutch performances, including a 26-point effort in Game 6, earned him the Finals MVP award.
- **2006 Western Conference Finals:** Nowitzki's performance in Game 7 against the San Antonio Spurs was legendary. He scored 37 points, including a game-tying three-pointer in the final seconds of regulation, to lead the Mavericks to victory and advance to the NBA Finals.
- **2011 Western Conference Semifinals:** In Game 1 against the Los Angeles Lakers, Nowitzki scored 48 points, showcasing his scoring prowess and leading the Mavericks to a crucial victory.
- **2011 NBA Playoffs:** The consistency and leadership he portrayed throughout the playoffs were instrumental in the Mavericks' championship run. His ability to elevate his game in high-pressure situations and deliver when it mattered most left a lasting impression on fans and peers.
- **2010-2011 Regular Season:** Dirk's performance during the regular season leading up to the championship year was exceptional. He averaged 23 points and 7 rebounds per game, solidifying his status as one of the league's premier players.
- **2014-2015 Regular Season:** He became the sixth player in NBA history to reach the 27,000-point milestone during this season, further cementing his place among the all-time greats.

Manu Ginóbili

Manu Ginobili, the basketball maestro from Argentina, touched hearts in the NBA with his unique playing style and the iconic Eurostep move. The Eurostep, a move that Manu popularized and mastered, became his signature on the NBA stage. This innovative maneuver involves a quick change of direction while driving to the basket, allowing the player to evade defenders and create scoring opportunities. Ginobili's execution of the Eurostep was a thing of beauty, as he seamlessly glided past opponents with grace and finesse.

Fans and fellow players alike marveled at his mastery of the Eurostep. His ability to deceive defenders with his footwork and create open lanes to the basket made him a formidable offensive threat. The Eurostep became synonymous with Ginobili's playing style, a symbol of his creativity on the court.

What set him apart was not just his flashy moves but also his competitiveness, basketball acumen, and clutch performances in critical moments. He was known for his fearless approach to the game, always being fearless and being willing to take risks and make plays when it mattered most. Throughout his career, the Eurostep became a feared weapon that opponents struggled to defend against. His ability to read the defense, anticipate their movements, and execute the Eurostep with precision made him a nightmare for defenders. Whether finishing at the rim or creating scoring opportunities for his teammates, Ginobili's Euro Step was a game-changer.

Ginobili's legacy as a dynamic player and innovator of the Eurostep will forever be etched in basketball history. His influence on the game moved beyond borders, inspiring a new generation of players to incorporate creativity and flair into their playing style.

Highlights of His Career

Manu's career is filled with many moments that established him as a force to be reckoned with. Some of his standout moments include:

1. **2005 NBA Finals Game 5:** His performance in Game 5 against the Detroit Pistons was spectacular. He scored 23 points off the bench, including a crucial three-pointer in the final seconds to seal the victory for the San Antonio Spurs and help them capture the NBA championship.
2. **2007 NBA playoffs:** his exceptional play throughout the playoffs, including a memorable performance in the Western Conference Finals against the Utah Jazz, where he scored 22 points in the fourth quarter to lead the Spurs to victory.
3. **2012 Olympics:** Manu represented Argentina in the 2012 London Olympics and played a pivotal role in leading his team to a bronze medal finish. His leadership, scoring ability, and all-around play were instrumental in Argentina's success on the international stage.
4. **2014 NBA Finals Game 5:** Ginobili's stellar performance in Game 5 against the Miami Heat, where he recorded 24 points, 10 assists, and 6 rebounds, showcased his versatility and impact on the court. His contributions helped the Spurs secure their fifth NBA championship.
5. **Career milestones:** Throughout his NBA career, Ginobili achieved numerous milestones, including being a two-time All-Star, winning four NBA championships with the San Antonio Spurs, and earning the Sixth Man of the Year award in 2008. His impact on the game extended beyond statistics, as he was known for his unselfish play, basketball IQ, and leadership on and off the court.

Yao Ming

Standing at 7 feet 6 inches tall, Yao Ming's journey from Shanghai, China, to the NBA stole the hearts of fans worldwide and inspired a generation of young basketball players in his home country.

Yao Ming's background is rooted in his early years in Shanghai, where he was born to basketball-playing parents. His exceptional height and talent for the game were evident from a young age, and he quickly rose through the ranks of Chinese basketball. Yao's father, Yao Zhiyuan, was a former professional basketball player, and his mother, Fang Fengdi, was a standout player on the Chinese national team. Their influence and guidance played a significant role in Yao Ming's development as a basketball prodigy.

He made history in 2002 as the first overall pick in the NBA Draft by the Houston Rockets, and the impact he made extended beyond the court, as he became a cultural icon and ambassador for the sport in China. His success in the NBA helped popularize basketball in China and sparked a surge of interest in the sport among Chinese youth. His dominant play, sportsmanship, and humility endeared him to fans around the world, defying cultural boundaries and uniting people through the universal language of basketball.

Yao Ming's influence on the development of basketball in China was profound. His presence in the NBA raised the profile of Chinese basketball on the global stage and inspired a new generation of players to pursue their dreams. The Yao Ming Foundation was established to support educational and humanitarian initiatives, further solidifying his commitment to making a positive impact in his community and beyond. It wasn't however always a smooth sailing journey, some of the challenges he faced along the way include:

- Cultural Adjustment: Moving from China to the United States presented Yao Ming with a significant cultural adjustment. Adapting to a new language, lifestyle, and environment posed challenges as he navigated a different social and professional landscape.
- Physical Demands: The NBA's fast-paced and physical style of play was a stark contrast to the basketball he was accustomed to in China. Yao Ming had to adjust to the speed, athleticism, and intensity of the NBA game, which required a different level of physical conditioning and skill set.
- Heightened Expectations: As the first overall pick in the NBA Draft, he faced immense pressure to perform at a high level and live up to the expectations set for him. The spotlight was on him to succeed and make an impact, adding to the challenges of transitioning to a new league and country.
- Language Barrier: Communication was a significant hurdle for him, as English was not his first language. Overcoming the language barrier posed challenges in understanding play calls, communicating with teammates and coaches, and acclimating to the NBA's English-speaking environment.
- Physicality and Competition: Adjusting to the physicality and competitiveness of NBA opponents was a learning curve for Yao Ming. He faced formidable opponents who tested his skills, strength, and endurance, requiring him to adapt his game and develop new strategies to succeed at the highest level of basketball.

Despite these challenges, he still worked as hard as he could to get to where he was. He reinforced the idea that your best efforts will always pay off for you in the end.

Yao's Achievements and Awards

Some of the awards that Yao received throughout his career include:

1. NBA All-Star Selections: Yao Ming was selected as an NBA All-Star eight times during his career, showcasing his popularity and recognition as one of the league's top players.
2. All-NBA Team Honors: Yao Ming was named to the All-NBA Team multiple times, recognizing his exceptional performance and contributions to the Houston Rockets.
3. NBA Rookie of the Year: In his debut season, Yao Ming was named the NBA Rookie of the Year, highlighting his impact and potential as a rising star in the league.
4. FIBA Basketball World Cup MVP: he was named the Most Valuable Player (MVP) of the FIBA Basketball World Cup, underscoring his dominance on the international stage.
5. Chinese Basketball Association (CBA) Championships: Yao Ming won multiple CBA championships with the Shanghai Sharks, solidifying his status as a successful player in his home country.
6. Olympic achievements: Yao represented China in multiple Olympic Games and played a key role in leading the national team to success, earning recognition for his contributions to Chinese basketball.
7. Basketball Hall of Fame induction: In recognition of his impact on the sport and his legacy as a basketball icon, he was inducted into the Naismith Memorial Basketball Hall of Fame, cementing his place among the all-time greats in basketball history.

We are who we are and we come from where we come from, but what defines us really is the effort and the work that we put in to chart our own path.

If anything, Dirk, Manu, and Yao show this to be true. We can't choose where we come from, but we still have the power to choose where we go from there.

CHAPTER 10: GOLD AND GLORY—THE RISE OF THE 2008 REDEEM TEAM

Aaah, the Beijing Olympics. I was still relatively young at that time, not too young though, but watching the sporting events was a way that my family and I connected. My mom would make us snacks, my favorite was homemade popcorn with a sprinkle of salt and a dash of butter. The whole family would gather around the TV, cheering for our favorite athletes and countries, feeling the thrill of victory and the agony of defeat together.

There's one particular evening that stands out in my memory. It was a quiet night, but the air filled with excitement as we tuned in to watch the basketball competition. The arena was buzzing with energy, the crowd roaring with anticipation. As the teams took to the court, I felt a surge of adrenaline, eager to witness the magic unfold. The game was intense, each possession filled with drama and suspense. The players moved with precision and grace, their skills on full display for the world to see. The stakes were high, and the competition fierce, but what captivated me the most was the spirit of unity and sportsmanship that permeated the event.

As the final moments of the game approached, the tension mounted. The score was close, but the outcome was uncertain. I held my breath, my heart pounding in my chest, as the players battled it out on the court. And then, in a flash of brilliance, a player rose to the occasion, delivering a game-changing play that would go down in Olympic history.

The buzzer sounded, the crowd erupted in cheers, and I sat there in awe of what I had just witnessed. It wasn't just about the victory or the defeat; it was about the journey, the passion, and the camaraderie that defined the Olympic spirit. In that moment, I felt a sense of pride and inspiration, knowing that anything was possible with hard work, dedication, and a belief in oneself.

What I learned at that moment, is that sports are about unity—uniting people from all walks of life, and the Beijing Olympics in particular, reminded me of the magic that happens when athletes come together to chase their dreams and strive for gold and glory.

On a Mission For Gold

The U.S. men's basketball team arrived at the 2008 Beijing Olympics with a mission to reclaim their dominance in the field and restore their reputation as a basketball powerhouse on the global stage. After facing setbacks in previous international competitions, the team was determined to showcase their talent, teamwork, and resilience in pursuit of gold.

They were led by head coach Mike Krzyzewski, affectionately known as Coach K, the team brought a strong sense of unity and purpose to their Olympic campaign. Coach K's leadership and strategic acumen were instrumental in fostering a cohesive team dynamic and instilling a winning mentality among the players. His emphasis on teamwork, communication, and mutual respect created a culture of excellence that propelled the team to success. Players like LeBron James, Kobe Bryant, Dwyane Wade, and Chris Paul brought their individual talents and leadership qualities to the team, forming a formidable lineup of stars. Their commitment to the collective goal of reclaiming gold for the United States was evident in their dedication to training, their on-court performances, and their unwavering support for one another.

Throughout the tournament, the team showcased their skill, athleticism, and competitive spirit, dominating their opponents with a combination of offensive firepower and defensive tenacity. Their chemistry on the court came alive through months of preparation and camaraderie; It was a testament to the work put in by Coach K and the coaching staff.

As the team advanced through the Olympic competition, each player embraced their role and contributed to the team's success in their own unique way. Whether it was LeBron James's versatility, Kobe Bryant's scoring prowess, or Dwyane Wade's clutch performances, every member of the team played a vital part in the journey to reclaiming gold and restoring U.S. basketball supremacy.

Key Matchups and Memorable Moments

During the 2008 Olympics, the men brought their all and gave it all they got, which is what made every game they played a sight to behold. Some of their key matchups and memorable moments included

- **Matchup Against Spain in the Gold Medal Game**: The final game against Spain was a tough battle for the U.S. team.

Spain put up a strong fight, but the U.S. team's teamwork and skill helped them secure a victory and claim the gold medal.
- **Semifinal Match Against Argentina**: In the semifinals, the U.S. team faced Argentina, a strong opponent with talented players like Manu Ginobili. The U.S. team's defense and offensive plays were outstanding, leading them to a decisive win and a spot in the gold medal game.
- **Kobe Bryant's Clutch Performances**: Kobe Bryant, known for his scoring ability and clutch plays, had several memorable moments during the 2008 Olympics. His leadership and scoring prowess were crucial in key matchups, inspiring his teammates and helping the team secure important victories.
- **LeBron James's Dominance**: LeBron James showcased his versatility and all-around skills throughout the tournament. His dominant performances, including powerful dunks and precise passes, were highlights of the U.S. team's journey to the gold medal.
- **Team Unity and Celebrations**: One of the most memorable aspects of the 2008 Olympics was the strong sense of unity and camaraderie among the U.S. team. Players celebrated victories together, supported each other on and off the court, and demonstrated a true team spirit that contributed to their success.

Lessons on Leadership

Good leaders are not just born, they're made from experience and growth. Here are some key lessons on leadership that we can all take wisdom from the U.S. Team during the 2008 Olympics.

- **Communicate effectively:** The U.S. men's basketball team demonstrated effective communication on the court through

coordinated plays, passing, and defensive strategies. Their ability to communicate and work together as a cohesive unit contributed to their success in key matchups.
- **Lead by example:** Players like Kobe Bryant and LeBron James led by example with their exceptional skills, work ethic, and determination during the season. Their leadership on the court inspired their teammates to elevate their performance and strive for excellence.
- **You must be adaptable:** The U.S. team displayed adaptability by adjusting their game plan based on the strengths and weaknesses of their opponents. Their ability to adapt to different playing styles and situations allowed them to overcome challenges and secure victories.
- **Empower others:** Coach Mike Krzyzewski empowered his players by fueling confidence in their abilities and trusting them to make decisions on the court. This empowerment fostered a sense of ownership and responsibility among the players, leading to a strong team dynamic.
- **Manage emotions:** The team showed emotional intelligence by maintaining composure, focus, and resilience in high-pressure situations. They didn't let emotions get the best of them. Their ability to manage their emotions, stay composed under stress, and support each other emotionally contributed to their success in critical moments.
- **Life is a continuous learning process:** The players and coaching staff welcomed new challenges, sought feedback, and adapted their strategies to improve and excel throughout the tournament, showing a commitment to ongoing development and success. As the saying goes: you don't get better by doing the same things over and over again.

CHAPTER 11: RAPTORS TAKE ON LAKERS IN L.A.

One of the most fascinating aspects of basketball is its intriguing origin story that traces back to the creative mind of Dr. James Naismith in 1891. Dr. Naismith, a dedicated physical education instructor, faced a challenge-how to keep his students active and engaged during the harsh winter months when outdoor activities were limited. Inspired by a desire to create a new indoor game that combined skill, strategy, and teamwork, he set out to invent what would become one of the most popular sports in the world.

Armed with a soccer ball, two peach baskets, and a vision for a game that would test both physical and mental abilities, Dr. Naismith embarked on a journey of innovation and experimentation. He carefully crafted a set of 13 basic rules that would govern this new game, each designed to promote fair play, sportsmanship, and a spirit of friendly competition among players.

On that fateful day in December, Dr. Naismith introduced his students to the game of basketball for the very first time. The objective was simple—score points by tossing the soccer ball into the peach baskets suspended at each end of the gymnasium. What began as a modest experiment soon blossomed into a thrilling and dynamic sport that captured the imagination of all who played and watched.

As the students dribbled, passed, and shot the ball with enthusiasm and determination, the essence of basketball was born. The sound of sneakers squeaking on the gym floor, the swish of the ball through the net, and the cheers of encouragement filled the air, creating an atmosphere of excitement and camaraderie that would define the sport for generations to come.

Dr. Naismith's innovative creation quickly gained popularity, spreading from school gyms to community centers and eventually to arenas and stadiums around the world. The simple yet revolutionary concept of basketball had taken root, captivating players and fans with its blend of athleticism, strategy, and teamwork. From its humble beginnings in a small gymnasium in Massachusetts, basketball had emerged as a global phenomenon, uniting people of all ages, backgrounds, and cultures in a shared love for the game.

A Tale of Two Teams

The Raptors and the Lakers were complete opposites in the world of basketball. The Lakers, a storied franchise with a rich history and a legacy of championship aspirations, stood as a beacon of success and excellence in the NBA. Led by iconic figures like Magic Johnson, Kareem Abdul-Jabbar, and Kobe Bryant, the Lakers had a tradition of greatness that spanned decades, with multiple championship titles and a reputation as one of the most successful teams in the league.

On the other hand, the Raptors were an emerging team, relatively new to the NBA landscape compared to the Lakers. Based in Toronto, Canada, the Raptors had a shorter history and fewer accolades compared to their counterparts in Los Angeles. Despite their status as a younger franchise, the Raptors were on a journey of growth and development, seeking to establish themselves as a competitive force in the league.

The Lakers' storied past was filled with iconic moments, legendary players, and a culture of winning that set them apart from other teams. Their championship aspirations were ingrained in the team's DNA, with a commitment to excellence and a relentless pursuit of success driving their every move. The Lakers' tradition of greatness cast a long shadow over the NBA, with fans and rivals alike recognizing them as a powerhouse in the league.

In contrast, the Raptors were writing a new chapter in their story, one filled with promise, potential, and a hunger for success. Despite facing challenges and setbacks along the way, the Raptors were building a foundation for future success, with a dedicated fan base and a resilient spirit that propelled them forward. Led by emerging stars like Kyle Lowry and DeMar DeRozan, the Raptors were on a mission to carve out their own place in NBA history.

As the Lakers and Raptors prepared to face off in a highly anticipated showdown, the stage was set for a clash of contrasting storylines. The Lakers, with their championship pedigree and lofty aspirations, represented a legacy of greatness and a tradition of excellence. The Raptors, with their budding talent and hunger for success, symbolized a new era of growth and potential in the NBA.

Despite their differences, both teams shared a common goal: to compete at the highest level, to inspire their fans, and to leave a lasting impact on the world of basketball. The tale of these two teams, with their divergent paths and shared passion for the game, showed the richness of the NBA landscape, where stories of triumph, perseverance, and hope unfolded on the hardwood night after night.

Fire on The CourT

When I say you had to be there—you had to be there for the epic showdown between the Raptors and the Lakers in 2006. The air sizzled with anticipation as the two teams took the court, each determined to claim victory in a game that would go down in basketball history. The jump ball began with a flurry of action, as both teams traded baskets and defensive stops in a fast-paced, high-energy showdown. The Raptors, fueled by their emerging talent and hunger for success, came out strong, while the Lakers, with their storied history and championship aspirations, fought back with tenacity and skill.

As the game progressed, the intensity reached a fever pitch, with dramatic twists and turns keeping fans on the edge of their seats. The Raptors, led by Kyle Lowry's sharpshooting and DeMar DeRozan's acrobatic drives to the basket, surged ahead, igniting the crowd with their electrifying play. But the Lakers, anchored by Kobe Bryant's scoring magical powers and Pau Gasol's dominant presence in the paint, refused to back down, mounting a fierce comeback that had fans roaring with excitement.

With each possession, the tension mounted, the stakes growing higher with every shot and defensive stand. The Raptors and Lakers traded blows, neither willing to concede an inch in a game that had become a battle of wills and skill. The clock ticked down, the score tied, as the final moments of the game approached, setting the stage for a heart-stopping finish that would leave fans breathless.

In the waning seconds of the game, with the outcome hanging in the balance, Kyle Lowry drove to the basket, weaving through defenders with finesse and determination. As he rose for a game-winning shot, the arena fell silent, the fate of the game resting on his shoulders. The ball left his fingertips, soaring through the air in a perfect arc, before swishing through the net as the buzzer sounded, sealing a thrilling victory for the Raptors and sending the crowd into a frenzy of cheers and celebration.

The Raptors had triumphed in a game for the ages, their grit shining through in a hard-fought battle against the Lakers. The intensity of the match, the dramatic twists and turns, and the sheer excitement of the moment made it a game that would be remembered for years to come. I mean look now, It's years later and I still remember that match as if it happened just hours ago.

Key Moments of The Match

There were tons of moments that stole the show that day, adding more to the excitement and intensity of the match.

- **Kyle Lowry's clutch three-pointer**: In a crucial moment late in the game, Kyle sank a deep three-pointer to give the Raptors the lead. His precision shooting under pressure ignited the crowd and shifted the momentum in favor of the Raptors.
- **DeMar DeRozan's slam dunk**: DeMar's thunderous slam dunk over a Lakers defender electrified the arena and showcased his athleticism and scoring ability. The highlight-reel play energized the Raptors and fired up the crowd.
- **Kobe Bryant's fadeaway Jumper**: Kobe, known for his scoring, hit a tough fadeaway jumper over multiple defenders, demonstrating his clutch gene and ability to

deliver in critical moments. The shot kept the Lakers in contention and showcased Bryant's skill and determination.
- **Pau Gasol's block**: Pau's crucial block on a Raptors player's layup attempt preserved the Lakers' lead and showcased his defensive prowess. The timely block shifted the momentum back in favor of the Lakers and highlighted Gasol's impact on both ends of the court.
- **Game-Winning layup**: In the final seconds of the game, a Raptors player drove to the basket and converted a game-winning layup as time expired. The decisive play sealed the victory for the Raptors and capped off a thrilling game filled with memorable moments and key plays.

There's always room for improvement—There may be someone more skilled, a team with more titles and accolades, but what truly matters is how committed you are to achieving the goal. In basketball and in life, focusing on your own progress and development can lead to success and fulfillment, the Lakers and Raptors are two prime examples of this truth right here. So whatever you do, go out there, show up as best as you can, and always give it your all, even if it does seem that you're going to come out last in the end.

CHAPTER 12: CLASH OF TITANS: CLEVELAND VS. GOLDEN STATE IN THE 2016 FINALS

So, one of my friends growing up had his own little tradition before he'd play a match. Honestly, I'm just really fascinated by how he would religiously make sure that he did the same thing before stepping out on the court, no matter how late he was running or how severely out of time he was. So he kept this tiny pocket bible in his locker, and before every game, he would take a moment to read a passage from it. The way he would close his eyes, bow his head, and find a sense of calm and focus in those words always intrigued me. It was like his pre-game ritual was more than just a routine—it was a source of strength and inspiration that helped him prepare mentally and emotionally for the challenges ahead.

As he tucked the pocket bible back into his locker, a sense of peace would wash over him, and he would step onto the court with quiet confidence and determination. I remember watching him play, his movements fluid and purposeful, his demeanor calm yet resolute. It was as if that brief moment of reflection and connection with something greater than himself had a profound impact on his performance.

And so, game after game, I witnessed the power of his pre-game ritual, the way it grounded him, centered him, and fueled his passion for the sport. It made me realize that in the middle of the fast-paced action and intense competition of basketball, there was also room for moments of quiet introspection, personal rituals, and inner strength. My friend's simple yet profound tradition taught me that sometimes, the smallest gestures can have the biggest impact and that finding and making time for peace and inspiration can be just as important as the physical preparation for a game.

The Big Match

Anyone and everyone who loves basketball was talking about that match, I tell you! The lead-up to the 2016 NBA Finals showdown between the Cleveland Cavaliers and the Golden State Warriors was nothing short of electric. It was a clash of titans, a battle between two powerhouse teams with contrasting styles of play that promised an epic showdown on the court.

The Golden State Warriors, known for their fast-paced, high-octane offense and sharpshooting prowess, were the defending champions and the team to beat. Led by the "Splash Brothers," Stephen Curry and Klay Thompson, the Warriors boasted a lethal combination of three-point shooting, ball movement, and defensive tenacity that had propelled them to the top of the league. On the other side, the Cleveland Cavaliers, led by LeBron James, brought a different style of play to the table. With a focus on physicality, defense, and LeBron's unparalleled ability to dominate in all facets of the game, the Cavaliers were a formidable opponent with a hunger for redemption after falling short in the previous year's Finals.

As the series unfolded, each game was filled with heart-stopping moments, jaw-dropping plays, and intense drama that kept fans on the edge of their seats. From LeBron's iconic chase-down blocks to Curry's dazzling three-pointers, the star power and skill on display were nothing short of mesmerizing.

One of the most memorable moments came in Game 7, the ultimate decider of the series. With the score tied and the clock winding down, LeBron James delivered a clutch block on Andre Iguodala's layup, a play that would go down in NBA history as one of the greatest defensive stops in Finals history. Moments later, Kyrie Irving drained a three-pointer that sealed the victory for the Cavaliers and brought the championship home to Cleveland. The contrasting styles of play between the Warriors and Cavaliers added a layer of intrigue and excitement to the series. The Warriors' fast-paced, perimeter-oriented offense clashed with the Cavaliers' physicality and defensive mindset, creating a dynamic and compelling matchup that showcased the best of both teams.

That 2016 NBA Finals between the Cleveland Cavaliers and the Golden State Warriors sure did live up to the hype and delivered a spectacle for the ages. The intensity, skill, and sheer drama of the series captivated fans around the world and solidified its place as one of the most memorable Finals matchups in NBA history.

Draymond Green's Suspension

As a key player for the Golden State Warriors Draymond's absence altered the dynamics of the series and shifted the balance of power between the Warriors and the Cleveland Cavaliers.

He was suspended for accumulating flagrant foul points throughout the playoffs, leading to an automatic one-game suspension. His absence in Game 5 disrupted the Warriors' defensive rotations, rim protection, and overall team chemistry. Without Green's defensive presence and playmaking abilities, the Warriors faced challenges in containing LeBron James, Kyrie Irving, and the Cavaliers' offense.

The Cavaliers capitalized on this, exploiting the void in the Warriors' defense and attacking the paint with increased aggression. LeBron James, in particular, took advantage of Green's absence to assert his dominance and lead the Cavaliers to a crucial victory in Game 5, shifting the momentum of the series in favor of Cleveland.

Green's suspension not only impacted Game 5 but also had lingering effects on subsequent games in the series. His absence disrupted the Warriors' rhythm and defensive strategies, forcing adjustments in rotations and matchups that affected the team's overall performance and cohesion on the court.

Key Moments of The Match

- **Kyrie Irving's clutch shot**: In Game 7, Kyrie Irving hit a game-winning three-pointer over Stephen Curry in the final minutes, showcasing his scoring ability and nerves of steel in high-pressure situations. The shot gave the Cavaliers a crucial lead and swung the momentum in their favor.
- **Draymond Green's suspension**: Draymond Green, a key player for the Warriors, was suspended for Game 5 of the series due to accumulating flagrant foul points. His absence had a deep impact on the Warriors' defense and overall team dynamics, shifting the balance of the series.
- **LeBron James' triple-double performances**: Throughout the series, LeBron James recorded multiple triple-doubles, demonstrating his versatility and impact on the game. His

ability to contribute in scoring, rebounding, and playmaking was instrumental in the Cavaliers' success.

- **Andre Iguodala's defensive efforts**: Andre Iguodala's defensive prowess and ability to guard LeBron James were crucial in limiting James' scoring opportunities and forcing tough shots. Iguodala's defensive contributions were key for the Warriors in containing the Cavaliers' offense.
- **Steve Kerr's coaching adjustments**: Warriors coach Steve Kerr made strategic adjustments throughout the series to counter the Cavaliers' game plan and exploit their weaknesses. His tactical decisions, lineup changes, and in-game adjustments played a significant role in shaping the outcome of the Finals.
- **The Warriors' record-breaking regular season**: Leading up to the Finals, the Warriors had a historic regular season, setting a new NBA record with 73 wins. Their dominance and success throughout the season added to the anticipation and excitement surrounding the Finals matchup against the Cavaliers.

CHAPTER 13: MICHAEL JORDAN—A LIVING, BREATHING, WALKING LEGEND

One of my all-time favorite movies is "Like Mike." The film follows the story of a young orphan who discovers a pair of magical sneakers that once belonged to a basketball legend. When he puts on the shoes, he gains extraordinary basketball skills and is able to play like his idol. The movie captures the essence of dreams coming true, the power of belief, and the impact that sports can have on a person's life.

As I watched the young boy navigate the challenges and triumphs of his newfound basketball talent, I was truly inspired by the message of perseverance, hard work, and belief in yourself. The magic of the sneakers, for me, symbolized the idea that with dedication, determination, and a little bit of luck, anything is possible. The film resonated with me on a personal level, reminding me sports are uplifting and motivating, and bring people together in pursuit of their dreams.

There is one scene in particular, one where Calvin is dribbling down the court, making game-winning shots, and inspiring his teammates with his newfound skills that left a lasting impression on me. It was a reminder that in the world of sports, as in life, passion, resilience, and a never-give-up attitude can lead to incredible achievements and moments of greatness.

"Like Mike" captured the magic of basketball, the joy of competition, and the self-discovery that comes with pursuing your passions. It reminded me that sometimes, all it takes is a belief in oneself and the courage to chase your dreams, no matter how impossible they may seem. The movie is a constant reminder to me of what we all have within us–that inherent capacity to achieve greatness.

Early Life and Career

Michael Jordan, one of the greatest basketball players of all time, had a remarkable journey that began in his early life and college career. Growing up in Wilmington, North Carolina, he discovered his love for basketball at a young age. His family played a significant role in nurturing his passion for the sport, with his father, James Jordan, serving as a source of inspiration and support.

As a high school student at Emsley A. Laney High School, Michael faced challenges because of his height but demonstrated exceptional talent and determination on the basketball court. His work passion, competitive spirit, and dedication to improving his skills set him apart from his peers and laid the foundation for his future success.

After high school, he went to the University of North Carolina at Chapel Hill, where he played college basketball under coach Dean Smith. During his time at UNC, his exceptional athleticism, scoring ability, and work ethic, earned him a reputation as a standout player in the Atlantic Coast Conference (ACC). One of the most iconic moments of his college career came during the 1982 NCAA Championship game against Georgetown. With just 17 seconds left on the clock, Jordan hit a game-winning jump shot that sealed the victory for UNC and solidified his status as a clutch performer. The championship win was a defining moment for Jordan and set the stage for his future success in basketball.

Off the court, he also shined academically and demonstrated leadership qualities that would serve him well throughout his career. His time at UNC not only honed his basketball skills but also instilled in him a strong work ethic, discipline, and a commitment to excellence that would define his professional journey in the NBA.

His early life and college career laid the groundwork for his future achievements and established him as a rising star in the world of basketball. His experiences at UNC shaped who he is at heart, setting the stage for the legendary career that would unfold in the NBA.

NBA Career Highlights

When I say that Michael came to steal the show, I really mean it. Throughout his illustrious career, Michael Jordan dazzled fans, inspired teammates, and left a lasting impact on the sport of basketball. Here are some of the highlights that defined his legendary career.

1. **Six NBA championships**: Michael Jordan led the Chicago Bulls to six NBA championships during the 1990s, establishing a dynasty and solidifying his legacy as one of the greatest winners in basketball history.
2. **Five MVP awards**: Jordan was a five-time NBA Most Valuable Player (MVP), recognizing his individual

excellence, leadership, and impact on the game. His MVP awards underscored his dominance and influence on the court.

3. **Ten Scoring titles**: Known for his insane scoring abilities, he won an impressive ten NBA scoring titles, showcasing his ability to put the ball in the basket with unmatched skill and precision.
4. **Clutch Performances:** Jordan was renowned for his clutch performances in critical moments, hitting game-winning shots, making key defensive stops, and elevating his game when it mattered most. His competitiveness and composure under pressure set him apart as a true basketball icon.
5. **Defensive excellence:** Beyond his offensive skills, Michael Jordan was also a standout defender, earning multiple All-Defensive Team selections and showcasing his ability to shut down opponents with his tenacity and basketball IQ.
6. **All-Star appearances:** Jordan was a 14-time NBA All-Star, representing the best of the best in the league and captivating audiences with his electrifying play and showmanship during All-Star Weekend.
7. **Hall of Fame induction:** In 2009, he was acknowledged in the Naismith Memorial Basketball Hall of Fame, recognizing his unparalleled contributions to the game and his enduring impact on basketball culture worldwide.
8. **Cultural icon:** Beyond his on-court achievements, Michael Jordan transcended sports to become a global cultural icon. His Air Jordan sneakers, his impact on fashion and popular culture, and his role as a philanthropist and businessman solidified his status as a larger-than-life figure in the world of sports and beyond.

Partnership With Nike for Air Force Brand

I can't write about Mike and not talk about sneakers. Do you like sneakers? Well, I saved up almost a year's worth of pocket money to get myself my first pair! His partnership with Nike on the Air Jordan brand changed sneaker culture and left and rocked the fashion and sports industries. The Air Jordan line, which debuted in 1985 with the release of the Air Jordan 1, transformed the way sneakers were perceived, turning them into coveted fashion statements and cultural icons.

So when he initially signed with Nike, he was given the opportunity to create his own signature shoe line, a groundbreaking concept at the time. The Air Jordan 1, with its bold design and innovative technology, was the essence of Jordan's style and personality both on and off the court. The unforgettable "Wings" logo and the "Air" cushioning system differentiated the line apart from other sneakers, making it an instant hit among fans and sneaker enthusiasts.

With each new Air Jordan release, excitement reached a fever pitch. Sneakerheads lined up for hours, eagerly awaiting the chance to own a piece of basketball history. I mean if you've also watched enough reality TV, you will know that there are people who dedicate whole rooms to their sneakers. The Air Jordan sneakers weren't just shoes. They were symbols of excellence, determination, and the relentless pursuit of greatness that Michael Jordan embodied. The brand in itself also wasn't just about sneakers; it was a cultural phenomenon that transcended sports.

The Jumpman logo became synonymous with style and success, while the Air Jordan colorways and designs set trends and influenced sneaker culture for generations to come. From the iconic Air Jordan 3 to the futuristic Air Jordan 11, each shoe told a story of innovation, creativity, and the impact that Mike has.

The Air Jordan brand became a lifestyle, a statement of individuality, and a connection to Jordan's unparalleled career in basketball. Fans didn't just wear Air Jordans; When they had the shoes on they carried the essence of greatness and excellence that Jordan represented.

Today, the brand is still as popular as it was when it first launched and it continues to thrive, with new releases, quirky audiences, and paying homage to the legacy of Michael Jordan. The Brand is a true symbol of passion and the enduring impact of one of the greatest basketball players of all time. Michael didn't just change the game of basketball; He changed the game of sneakers, leaving a mark on sneaker culture that is going to be seen and remembered by countless more generations.

Before wrapping up I want you to Remember that you are not going to get where you want to be if you are not willing to bet on yourself. If you're constantly on the sidelines waiting for other people to make space for you, you may miss out on opportunities to shine and reach your full potential. Believe in your abilities, take risks, and trust in your journey. The path to success begins with self-confidence, determination, and a willingness to step into the spotlight and show the haters what you're capable of, here are a few quotes by Michael to keep you inspired.

- "I've missed more than 9000 shots in my career. I've lost almost 300 games. 26 times, I've been trusted to take the game-winning shot and missed. I've failed over and over and over again in my life. And that is why I succeed."
- "Talent wins games, but teamwork and intelligence win championships."
- "I can accept failure, everyone fails at something. But I can't accept not trying."
- "I've always believed that if you put in the work, the results will come."

- "Obstacles don't have to stop you. If you run into a wall, don't turn around and give up. Figure out how to climb it, go through it, or work around it."
- "You have to expect things of yourself before you can do them."
- "I play to win, whether during practice or a real game. And I will not let anything get in the way of me and my competitive enthusiasm to win."
- "The game has its ups and downs, but you can never lose focus of your individual goals and you can't let yourself be beat because of lack of effort."
- "To be successful you have to be selfish, or else you never achieve. And once you get to your highest level, then you have to be unselfish. Stay reachable."

CONCLUSION

You will probably roll your eyes when you read this, but I really want to say that so much of what I know about life, I have learned through basketball.

You probably know by now through all of these stories that I have been telling throughout the book that when I was a kid, basketball was just a game to me. It was something I did with my friends on the playground, something I watched on TV with my dad and granddad. But as I got older, it became more than that. It became a passion, a way of life. Basketball taught me about the power of teamwork, and about working with others to achieve a common goal. It taught me about perseverance, about pushing through even when things are tough. It taught me about discipline, and about putting in the time and effort to improve. I am who I am because of this incredible game.

But perhaps most importantly, it taught me about the power of dreams. As a kid, I dreamed of being a basketball player. I practiced every day, worked hard, and eventually earned a spot on my high school team. I wasn't a star player by any means, but I loved being a part of the team and contributing in any way I could.

Basketball also taught me that dreams can change. As I got older, I realized that while I loved playing the game, I wasn't good enough to play at a higher level. Instead, my dream shifted to writing about basketball, sharing stories, and inspiring others to love the game as much as I do.

And that's what this book was all about. It's about sharing the stories of those who have achieved greatness on the court and inspiring the next generation of basketball players to dream big and work hard. So, as we wrap up this book, I want to say thank you to basketball. Thank you for teaching me so much about life. Thank you for inspiring me to dream big. And thank you for introducing me to so many incredible people, both on and off the court.

I hope that the stories in this book inspire you as much as they have inspired me. And I hope that, like me, you will continue to learn from basketball, long after the final buzzer has sounded. Keep well. Keep dreaming, and stay as incredible as you are.

References

Ayd, G. (n.d.). *NBA Golden era ending? Phil Jackson looks to exit with fourth "three Peat."* Bleacher Report. https://bleacherreport.com/articles/688295-nba-golden-era-ending-phil-jackson-looks-to-exit-with-fourth-three-peat

Beck, H. (2013, June 8). *The titles he won, the things they lost.* The New York Times. https://www.nytimes.com/2013/06/09/sports/basketball/the-games-tim-duncan-won-the-things-other-stars-have-lost.html

Beslic, S. (2021, February 6). *10 Things you didn't know about Kareem Abdul Jabbar.* Basketball Network - Your Daily Dose of Basketball. https://www.basketballnetwork.net/latest-news/10-things-you-didnt-know-about-kareem-abdul-jabbar

Boston Celtics vs Los Angeles Lakers rivalry. (n.d.). SportSkeeda. https://www.sportskeeda.com/basketball/boston-celtics-los-angeles-lakers-rivalry

Bowen, F. (2017, February 16). *In its early years, the NBA blocked black players.* The Washington Post. https://www.washingtonpost.com/lifestyle/kidspost/in-nbas-early-years-black-players-werent-welcome/2017/02/15/664aa92e-f1fe-11e6-b9c9-e83fce42fb61_story.html

Bryce-Saddler, M. (2020, February 24). *Kobe didn't watch his 81-point game for years — and hated "the easy shots" he missed.* Washington Post. https://www.washingtonpost.com/history/2020/02/24/kobe-bryant-81-point-game/

Buerge, D. (2020, June 10). *A complete timeline of the Shaq and Kobe feud.* Lakers Nation. https://lakersnation.com/a-complete-timeline-of-the-shaquille-oneal-kobe-bryant-feud/

Clemente, A. (2022, June 13). *NBA Finals: who is Ime Udoka, the coach who has revived the Celtics?* Diario AS. https://en.as.com/nba/nba-finals-who-is-ime-udoka-the-coach-who-has-revived-the-celtics-n/

Cleveland Cavaliers vs Golden State Warriors Jun 19, 2016 game summary. (n.d.). Www.nba.com. Retrieved February 29, 2024, from https://www.nba.com/game/cle-vs-gsw-0041500407

Cline, K. (2020, June 5). *Houston Rockets: How the team ruined a strong narrative in the 95 NBA Finals.* House of Houston. https://houseofhouston.com/2020/06/05/houston-rockets-hakeem-olajuwon-shaq-team-narrative-1995-finals/4/

Dimitri. (n.d.). *Top 50 Michael Jordan quotes About basketball and life.* Basketball mindset training https://www.basketballmindsettraining.com/blog/michael-jordan-quotes

Flannery, R. (2023, October 30). *NBA Icon Yao Ming sees international exchanges helping young Chinese basketball talent.* Forbes. https://www.forbes.com/sites/russellflannery/2023/10/30/nba-icon-yao-ming-sees-intl-exchanges-helping-young-chinese-basketball-talent/?sh=6e8db5866b7a

From Our Archives: *How Shaq and Kobe's Rivalry Shaped the Lakers.* (2020, January 28). LAmag - Culture, Food, Fashion, News & Los Angeles. https://lamag.com/featured/kobe-shaq-lakers-2001

Gennero, G. (2023, May 4). *Sports take: Tim Duncan is a top-five NBA player of all time.* The Baylor lariat.

https://baylorlariat.com/2023/05/04/sports-take-tim-duncan-is-a-top-five-nba-player-of-all-time/

Greer, J. (2019, March 2). *Five things you didn't know about Wilt Chamberlain's 100-point game.* Sportingnews.com. https://www.sportingnews.com/us/nba/news/wilt-chamberlain-100-points-game-stats-video-highlights-nba-records-knicks-warriors/1cgvr5xgyxdyr15hr3on0bqywk

Greer, J. (2022, August 8). *30 years later: How the "Dream Team" forever changed the NBA by opening doors for international players.* Sporting News. https://www.sportingnews.com/us/nba/news/dream-team-international-players-nba-30-years/wvtkr28hh1jgjhxmfotl9lqn

Hale, T. (2014, May 20). Tim Duncan isn't talking. Pounding the Rock. https://www.poundingtherock.com/2014/5/20/5735544/tim-duncan-silence

Hanning, T. (2020, February 20). *The mystique was dead: 1999-2000 Boston Celtics in review.* The Roar. https://www.theroar.com.au/2020/02/21/the-mystique-was-dead-1999-2000-boston-celtics-in-review/

Hansford, C. (2023, January 22). *This day in Lakers history: Kobe Bryant scores 81 points against the Raptors.* Lakers Nation. https://lakersnation.com/this-day-in-lakers-history-kobe-bryant-scores-81-points-against-raptors/

History of basketball. *Events, dates, people, & facts.* (2023, October 16). Brittanica https://www.britannica.com/sports/history-of-basketball

Hoops and laughter: The Harlem globetrotters | American experience | PBS. (2018, June 7).

PBShttps://www.pbs.org/wgbh/americanexperience/features/hoops-and-laughter-harlem-globetrotters/

Huq, R. (n.d.). *Why the the clutch City Rockets still thrive in today's NBA*. Chron. https://www.chron.com/sports/rockets/article/90s-rockets-nba-blueprint-17493833.php

Kareem Abdul-Jabbar. (n.d.). Academy of Achievement. https://achievement.org/achiever/kareem-abdul-jabbar/

Kareem Abdul-Jabbar sats. (2019). Basketball Reference. https://www.basketball-reference.com/players/a/abdulka01.html

Kareem Abdul-Jabbar: Los Angeles Lakers. (n.d.). NBA. https://www.nba.com/stats/player/76003/career

Klein, C. (2018, August 23). *10 things you may not know about the Harlem Globetrotters.* HISTORY. https://www.history.com/news/10-things-you-may-not-know-about-the-harlem-globetrotters

Legends profile: Michael Jordan. (2021, September 14). NBA. https://www.nba.com/news/history-nba-legend-michael-jordan

Litzky, F. (1999, October 12). *Wilt Chamberlain is dead at 63.* Archive.nytimes.com. https://archive.nytimes.com/www.nytimes.com/library/sports/basketball/101399bkn-obit-chamberlain.html

Mahoney, R. (2016, June 19). *How the imperfect Cavaliers dethroned the Warriors.* Sports Illustrated. https://www.si.com/nba/2016/06/20/lebron-cavs-pull-unthinkable-dethroning-warriors-title

Mantage, Y. (2020, June 7). *This date in NBA history (June 7): Rockets record 20-point comeback win in overtime to clinch game 1 of 1995 NBA finals vs. Magic and more.* Sporting News Canada. https://www.sportingnews.com/ca/houston-rockets/news/this-date-in-nba-history-june-7-rockets-record-20-point-comeback-win-in-overtime-to-clinch-game-1-of-1995-nba-finals-vs-magic-and-more/n66du4ynvcge156it7amawcwg

Manu Ginobili: Looking back on a career that changed the game of basketball. (n.d.). FIBA.basketball. https://www.fiba.basketball/news/manu-ginobili-looking-back-on-a-career-that-changed-the-game-of-basketball

McCallum, J. (n.d.). *In 2004 playoffs, star-studded Lakers' breakup seemed inevitable.* Sports Illustrated Vault https://vault.si.com/vault/2004/05/17/the-center-cannot-hold-a-game-3-rout-of-san-antonio-kept-las-title-hopes-alive-but-win-or-lose-this-is-the-last-stand-for-these-lakers

McGreggor, G. (2024, January 14). *How long was Draymond Green suspended? Explaining NBA's reinstatement of Warriors star after indefinite suspension.* Sporting News. https://www.sportingnews.com/us/nba/news/draymond-green-suspended-indefinite-warriors/bf9f4bf93e1db1fe727a98c9

Michael Jordan. (n.d.). Olympics. https://olympics.com/en/athletes/michael-jordan

Michael Jordan quotes. (2019). BrainyQuote. https://www.brainyquote.com/authors/michael-jordan-quotes

Michael Jordan quotes (author of driven from within). (2019). Goodreads.com. https://www.goodreads.com/author/quotes/16823.Michael_Jordan

Neuharth-Keusch, A. J. (2016, June 20). 2016 NBA finals: Warriors vs. Cavaliers. USA TODAY. https://www.usatoday.com/story/sports/nba/playoffs/2016/05/30/nb

a-finals-preview-warriors-cavaliers-stephen-curry-lebron-james/85173782/

Reggie Miller. (n.d.). TV Guide. https://www.tvguide.com/celebrities/reggie-miller/bio/3000077339/

Reggie Miller - Indiana Pacers shooting guard. (n.d.). ESPN. https://africa.espn.com/nba/player/_/id/552/reggie-miller

Ryan , B. (2022, June 1). *With the Celtics going for No. 18, here's a look back at their first 17 championships.* Boston Globehttps://www.bostonglobe.com/2022/06/01/sports/with-celtics-going-no-18-heres-look-back-their-first-17-championships/

S, I. (2023, February 18). *Top 10 Facts about Wilt Chamberlain.* Discover Walks Blog. https://www.discoverwalks.com/blog/united-states/top-10-facts-about-wilt-chamberlain/

Simmons, B. (n.d.). *Career Arc: Tim Duncan.* https://grantland.com/features/tim-duncan-part-1/

Starjacki, W. (2018, June 7). *Remembering game 1 of the 1995 NBA Finals.* Basketball Network - Your Daily Dose of Basketball. https://www.basketballnetwork.net/old-school/remembering-game-1-of-the-1995-nba-finals

The most prominent achievements Of Michael Jordan. (n.d.). Edubirdie. https://edubirdie.com/examples/the-most-prominent-achievements-of-michael-jordan/

The Naismith memorial basketball hall of fame: Phil jackson. (n.d.). Hoop Hall. https://www.hoophall.com/hall-of-famers/phil-jackson/

The Naismith Memorial Basketball Hall of Fame: Wilt Chamberlain. (n.d.). Hoop Hall. https://www.hoophall.com/hall-of-famers/wilt-chamberlain/

Tim Duncan promises to be "on The Court". (2015, July 3). CbS news https://www.cbsnews.com/texas/news/tim-duncan-promises-to-be-on-the-court/

Toole, C. (2023, August 25). *How the rockets staged the most improbable title run in NBA history.* BroBible. https://brobible.com/sports/article/houston-rockets-nba-title-1995/

Toronto Raptors vs Los Angeles Lakers Jan 22, 2006 box scores. (n.d.). NBa. https://www.nba.com/game/tor-vs-lal-0020500591/box-score

Watson, M. (2017, May 31). Everything you need to know about the 2016 NBA Finals. SBNation. https://www.sbnation.com/nba/2017/5/31/15715474/warriors-vs-cavs-2016-nba-finals-scores-results

Wolfman-Arent, A. (2022, March 2). *On the 60th anniversary, why Wilt Chamberlain's 100-point game still matters.* WHYY. https://whyy.org/articles/100-was-a-monument-60-years-later-wilt-chamberlains-record-still-inspires-awe/

Wright, M. (2016, July 13). *Fun out of fundamental: Duncan explains choice.* ESPN.com. https://www.espn.com/nba/story/_/id/17056716/tim-duncan-san-antonio-spurs-says-playing-fun-anymore

Yang, A. (2020, February 19). *Black history month: The Harlem Globetrotters changed basketball.* Sports Illustrated. https://www.si.com/nba/2020/02/19/black-history-month-harlem-globetrotters-lakers

Yao ming - houston rockets center. (n.d.). ESPN. https://africa.espn.com/nba/player/_/id/1722/yao-ming

Yao Ming : Biography & facts. (2018). In Encyclopædia Britannica. https://www.britannica.com/biography/Yao-Ming

Yiu, E. (2023, October 9). *19 unbelievable facts about Reggie Miller.* Facts.net. https://facts.net/celebrity/19-unbelievable-facts-about-reggie-miller/

Images

FreePik. (n.d.-a). *Abdul Jabbar dunk to the basketball* [Image]. http://freepik.com/ai/image-editor

FreePik. (n.d.-b). *Basketball Tim Duncan illustration* [Image]. http://freepik.com/ai/image-editor

FreePik. (n.d.-c). *Cleveland vs Golden State basketball match.* [Image]. http://freepik.com/ai/image-editor

FreePik. (n.d.-d). *General basketball Yao Ming height.* [Image]. http://freepik.com/ai/image-editor

FreePik. (n.d.-e). *General Shaquille and Kobe illustration* [Image]. http://freepik.com/ai/image-editor

FreePik. (n.d.-f). *Generic basketball image* [Image]. http://freepik.com/ai/image-editor

FreePik. (n.d.-g). *Illustration of Boston Celtics 1969* [Image]. http://freepik.com/ai/image-editor

FreePik. (n.d.-h). *Illustration of Harlem Globetrotters* [Image]. http://freepik.com/ai/image-editor

FreePik. (n.d.-i). *Illustration of Huston Rockets.* [Image]. http://freepik.com/ai/image-editor

FreePik. (n.d.-j). *Illustration of Reggie Miller* [Image]. http://freepik.com/ai/image-editor

FreePik. (n.d.-k). *Illustration of Wilt Chaimberlain* [Image]. http://freepik.com/ai/image-editor

FreePik. (n.d.-l). *Michael Jordan Illustration* [Image]. http://freepik.com/ai/image-editor

FreePik. (n.d.-m). *Raptors basketbball team 2006* [Image]. http://freepik.com/ai/image-editor

FreePik. (n.d.-n). *USA basketball Illustration* [Image]. http://freepik.com/ai/image-editor

Basketballs Background Illustration Designed by Freepik.

Printed in Great Britain
by Amazon